Disciplines for Life
in the
AGE OF
AQUARIUS

Disciplines for Life
in the
AGE OF
AQUARIUS

by LANCE WEBB

WORD BOOKS, Publisher
Waco, Texas

Disciplines for Life in the Age of Aquarius
by Lance Webb

Copyright © 1972 by Word, Incorporated
Waco, Texas 76703

Library of Congress catalog card number: 71–183342
Printed in the United States of America

DEDICATED

to my wife and life companion, Elizabeth,
whose giving-love in acceptance of me in all
my imperfections has revealed over and over
to me the Accepting Love deep in the heart
of all things

Contents

Preface

"Why would you want to write a book entitled *Disciplines for Life in the Age of Aquarius?*"

The question is reasonable and deserves an honest answer, but to answer it I must unveil my deepest struggles and become vulnerable. I must give my own personal story—a witness to the unquestionable fact that I would not be alive today with anything resembling creativity, joy, and value in my life and work without realizing two things.

First, the agony and despair that results from an undisciplined faith. That is, I had possessed meanings and purposes for my life in which I believed with the top of my mind but which had never been accepted and were often disobeyed by my deeper self. Like so many of my contemporaries who seek to live by a faith in someone or something bigger than they, I was a divided person. Part of me, consciously, most of the time, wanted to live by my ideals and convictions, while the deeper part of me rebelled. This split caused me to contradict and sometimes defy these convictions, bringing sorrow and self-disgust.

For several years I could easily have joined W. Somerset Maugham who said of himself, "There are times when I look over the various parts of my character with perplexity. I recognize that I am made up of several persons and that the person that at the moment has the upper hand will inevitably give place to another. But which is the real one? All of them or none?" As for me, I earnestly wanted to live by these fine ideals and values, but when the tests of life came, I was often weak, shifting, and inadequate. This was true

7

of me as a person, a husband, a father, as well as a minister-pastor-preacher in a Christian church.

Now this is an unexpected confession from one who has reached a "top" position by the standards of success generally accepted in the church as well as in the world. There are many who will say to me, "Surely you are not going to lay bare your failures, your doubts, your despairs, your anxieties and timidities! You have got to put up a better front than that if you want people to look to you!" Thus the world and the little ego within tell me. But here is the truth: I am painfully and wonderfully human—if you can take the paradox! And so are you. You too have phony masks to remove. But like me and anyone else who begins to find a life that is authentic and worth living in this exciting but dangerous world, you will have to see your masks, recognize them for what they are, and strip them off. This was and is my first necessity for life, as it is yours.

The second thing I have come to realize about my life has resulted in a growing experience of new insight into my true self and the real world in which I live and the courageous ability to live by these new found insights. This has been a costly experience indeed, like dying. For the old, phony selves have to die. But without this second realization, the first (the realization of my splintered, divided self) would have destroyed my effectiveness and left me in despair as it has countless thousands who simply couldn't face their own messes and musses with the unworthy fears, hostilities, and feelings of inadequacy and pride that caused them. To this second realization I owe whatever creativity and aliveness there is in Lance Webb today. This is the story I am telling in this book. I am describing the priceless discovery that if I was to become the true Lance Webb that I believe an eternally creative and loving Source and Ground of all life made me to be, I would have to take time to discipline my unconscious mind and spirit. I would be required in the very nature of my human life to take this time whether I thought I had it or not, whether I felt like it or not. I would do this through the regular, intelligent, faithful use of my conscious mind in discovering who I am, what my resources are, and in using the most priceless gift of human life, the great "I will," to be my authentic self in the service of others. All of this would be done in response to the Creator-Spirit who, I believe, is leading me to my life's fulfillment.

8

In my attempt to live by the faith I professed, I began to understand and practice these disciplines more thoroughly than previously I had ever understood as necessary. Until I saw the necessity of the disciplines of mind and spirit and until I had accepted and begun to practice them, I had been a sometime free person and an oftimes enslaved person. I was a struggler who lost as many battles as I won. I don't win them all now. Be sure of that. But on a January day in 1947 I decided my commitment of faith wasn't worth anything unless it was accompanied by a commitment to the disciplines that would enable me to live that faith day by day. From that time I have lived increasingly on tiptoe. There have been moments, hours, and occasionally a day or several days when I neglected the disciplines and slipped back into the old futilities and conflicts. But even during these recent years on the rack of arduous and urgent responsibilities, my life has become increasingly free and meaningful. I still have a long way to go, but I know the way and have traveled it for many years with more joy than I could ever have dreamed possible.

When I first began trying to live by a conscious faith, I was as sincere and dedicated a person as any mixed-up young man could be who had grown up with a lot of scars on his subconscious mind. I was fighting for the approval of my peers. When I left the one-teacher school where my father taught me until I was thirteen, I had to become a person in a rather frightening world. I was struggling to discover my true self and my mission, if I had one. Like a baby chicken I was trying to pip the shell which hid me from freedom and life within me and outside of me. I had to crawl out of my self-imposed lines of defense to see what this great, wide, wonderful world and its Creator had for me.

My first two years in college I spent seeking some identity as a reporter on the college newspaper and as solo trumpeter for the college band. Then on Easter Sunday, 1929, I came to a realization that gave me a great spurt of personal growth in creativity and freedom. I was not in church that Sunday because church for me was rather dull and I had other things to do. The Christian beliefs I had been taught as a child were in a state of suspension. That afternoon as I tried to help my roommate meet a crisis in his life, I faced a sudden question—*what was my life for anyway?* And I knew that the realities of my parents' faith and the faith of some

9

others I had known would have to be reckoned with in addition to the realities of physics and chemistry and the biological urges I felt so strongly.

That day I decided there was only one thing that would produce the peace and loving cooperation so desperately needed in my home, in my society, and in my country, which at that time was in the beginning of the depression. The one thing needed most, I concluded, was the wholehearted conviction or faith that puts us in the frame of the family of God as Jesus Christ had revealed him. This was my moment of decision to study for the Christian ministry and to do all I could to participate in a spiritual awakening. Even then I was convinced that this needed renewal of human life was coming, and that if it didn't we would be in a mess. I wanted to have a part in the awakening and not in the mess. And that was before the atom bomb, World War II, Korea, Vietnam, pollution, population explosion, and the great but frightening developments of "megatechnology"!

For the next seventeen years I struggled to get out of my selfish cocoon and grow into a mature person. I fought the battle of faith and doubt, of selfishness and self-giving, of love and hate. The battle went on all through college and graduate school and continued even as I tried to preach in little churches which my father and other trusting pastors provided. The struggle continued as I went to my first assignment—the organizing and building of two new churches in an oil-field town in West Texas. Here my high-flung, idealistic philosophy and theology were tried and found wanting, though the strong ardor of my struggle to proclaim the Good News of the Christian faith did produce some results. After a year as chaplain of McMurry College, four years as pastor in Shamrock, and one year in Eastland, Texas, I was appointed to continue a newly begun ministry in University Park, Dallas. During these years I had a taste of what all young men and women experience when they go out, handicapped by a divided self, to win a worthy battle. I was completely committed, I thought, to being the best man I could be as the husband of a lovely wife and the father of three little girls, as a citizen of a good country, and as the pastor of a church that was growing so rapidly we were in a state of perpetual crisis.

Because I threw myself so completely into my life and work, I had some high moments of success and of personal victory over

10

my inauthentic self. But I also had times when I almost gave up in despair. I would pray and read, seeking for help, and come out with a burst of new freedom and creativity. But after a few days I would sink back into the same old rut of insecurity and into what occasionally would have to be called by its true name, envy and jealousy, as I compared myself with other ministers who had opportunities I thought I could handle as well or better than they. But here I was with this church and its challenging opportunities as well as its harassing problems and needs. I loved people and spent many hours ministering to them out of genuine concern, but one day I had the shock of my life.

One of my good friends sat down in my office and said to me, "Lance, we know you love us, but some of us wonder whether or not you are more concerned about getting this church built than with us!"

Those words pierced my very soul. I could not get away from them as I sat a few days later in a meeting with other pastors and heard a very effective preacher talk about the necessity for "getting oneself off one's hands." That morning as I listened and as we closed the meeting, I made the second most momentous decision of my life. I had previously committed myself to follow Christ as best I understood him, but I had never committed myself to regular disciplines of prayer, reading, and thinking in the presence of God, nor had I been willing to submit myself to the discipline of a group with the same goal. Arriving home, I told my wife and my secretary that from that day on the first thirty minutes or hour in my study every morning was to be given to the one purpose of meeting the truth of Christ and "getting my false self off my hands." However long it took, I was determined to find the resources and the insights I needed to fulfill my life and ministry. Nothing was to interfere except an unusual emergency in the life of one of my people or my own family.

Since that day in January, 1947, I have kept that commitment as faithfully as I could. From it and from other disciplines which will be described in this book have come a discovery of the most important things in my life today. Among these is the whole new world of autobiographical literature containing the experiences of vital persons in every age. I hadn't known such resources existed. Here I found mirrored in their lives my own struggles and problems.

11

I also saw the practical outworking of the deeper meanings of trust and love which Christ revealed. Here I met the undergirding challenge of the love of God that shone in Jesus Christ calling me to learn to trust and love others.

I discovered the means by which I could come through the low places when feelings and misgivings were all running contrary to my conscious faith. Here I received the power to come through what other Christians have called "the dark night of the soul," when outward circumstances and the cynical atheism of the world in which I lived sought to throw me off the track.

The wonderful part is that the intervals between the low places of doubt and depression were much farther apart as they were met with renewed faith and greater insights. I knew with Paul that "when I am weak then I am strong." I began, what has been for me, one of the most helpful disciplines in my entire life. In a book with a blank page for every day in the year, I wrote down the selections from the Scripture, the experiences of some other seeker after truth, a poem, the verse of a hymn, or the honest description of what was taking place within me. Generally, I would read until I came upon a sentence or a paragraph that really spoke to me. I recorded the selection in my own poor handwriting (which most people can't read), and then I wrote my appropriate response. Sometimes it was a confession. At other times there were insights into why I failed and decisions as to what I was to do about the situation I was facing. Often it was to write my new commitment, my new trust, and my thanksgiving and praise for the One in whose presence I can truthfully say, "I have strength for anything through him who gives me power" (Phil. 4:13, NEB).

These books—one for each year since—reflect the story of my pilgrimage through the difficult testings and opportunities that have come to me—the weary burdens I have borne, the triumphant experiences of victory over my phony self-demands, the equally triumphant experience of sharing with others who were winning the victory of faith. I can turn back through these books and trace the crises by which my faith has grown and the divisions and conflicts within my subconscious mind which have been increasingly overcome.

If a fire were to start in my home, the first things I would seek to save would be these living-the-faith notebooks. They are precious to me for what they represent—the way in which the Spirit of Christlike love has led me, fighting and kicking much of the time, out of myself and into a life that is freer and more creative than I ever dreamed it could be.

So behind the pages that follow is this experience which I have shared in bare outline. I have not won all the battles. I still doubt at times, but I believe with an infinitely greater assurance than ever that there is a well of grace springing up into life eternal at the heart of my now and of my future as well. I believe there is nothing more wonderful than having some buckets with which to draw from this deep well of life and the readiness to use these buckets regularly and thankfully. Life's greatest joys come when caringly, lovingly I am able to help some of my brothers and sisters in God's great family whom I may touch to drink and eat and live!

I write this not with the expectancy or the desire that you will try to follow exactly the same approaches I have made. I know this is impossible, for each of us is wonderfully but peculiarly made. But I do earnestly hope that these experiences and insights may do for you what others have done for me—point to the Well of Life and help you to find and use the buckets!

I

A New Song
for a
New Age

1 Meeting the Crisis of Faith

"Is there any purpose in life?" She was a tired, bedraggled youth who had run away from home. She had tried all the promises of freedom to do as she pleased from sex, to drugs, to organized protest against the evils she had seen on television and in her own sordid acquaintance with human failures.

She is part of the serious and often joyless generation that has grown up in a secular age with an overabundance of knowledge and skills in the "how-tos" and very little understanding of the "whys" and "why-nots."

Millions like her today have not, however, visibly and outwardly run away. Like her they are empty, fed up, tired of life's meaninglessness which all our scientific know-how cannot touch. Like her, we have all existed in a mounting crisis of faith. There are, of course, varying degrees in our belief: some with a glimpse only, some with none, a few with strong and joyous convictions but conscious of rising doubts and confusion that threaten what joy we have known. What can anyone say to help her and all of us in this amazingly productive and yet fearfully destructive age?

In his disturbing book *The Myth of the Machine—the Pentagon of Power,* Lewis Mumford asks the gnawing question of how it happens that with all our advance in knowledge we seem to be arriving so quickly at a world "fit only for machines to live in."[1] Mr. Mumford attributes our condition to the worship of technology. He traces the way we arrived from "the unfortunate consequences of Galileo's (unconscious) 'crime' " that would "displace all traditional values and reject all experience and knowledge that did not conform" to the patterns of a machine.[2] He describes the way by

17

which the scientist, beginning with Descartes, became absolute
lawgiver and how Francis Bacon extended "the scientific method
to every department of life" with the "final goal of science . . . the
effecting of all things possible"[3] without foreseeing the consequent
harmful and antihuman events of the conquest of nature. He suggests
that the worship of technology brings us now to the point where
those of us who are aware at all can understand and shudder at
the "technological possibilities [which] are irresistible to man." As
the mathematician von Neumann described them, *"If man has the
power to exterminate all life on earth, he will."*[4]

Will he? Obviously with all the tremendous contributions of
science to the comfort and well-being of man, this science applied
to technics has indeed given us the power to exterminate all life
on earth through poisonous pollution, through waste of our natural
resources, and through atomic destruction either by war or by
radiation. Will we?

Yes, we will unless we discover the spiritual imperative that leads
us to find the *new song that celebrates and proclaims the faith from
which comes the meaning, value, hope, and responsible love necessary for human life in the age of megatechnics!* Many people have
lost the meaning and values of life as we once knew it. *Future Shock*
is already upon us, writes Alvin Toffler, in rapidly changing codes
of morality and modes of living—in transience, mobility, novelty—
with resulting fractured families and new forms of communal and
sexual relationships. It is upon us in "overstimulation, bombardment
of the senses, information overload, decision stress"[5]—all of which
are leading us to a collision course with the future. The present
conditions and the prophecies of his book are indeed frightening
for all who would like to believe that today's education will "fit
their children for life in the future"[6] and that scientific progress
inevitably brings the good life.

Add all this to our own personal crises—understanding our own
roles in life, conflicts within our families and communities, and it
is easy to see why people are shocked into apathy and immobility in
trying to believe that anything can be done to change our human
situation.

I think of several brilliant, gifted young Christian pastors in my
own episcopal area who, along with hundreds of priests and other
persons once dedicated to the belief that their services would make

a difference, have given up their jobs and quit trying. I have sat down and shared with several of them their agony of frustration and futility. Given their loss of hope and meaning, I could not blame them for quitting the ministry of the church.

Along with them are thousands of lay dropouts, not only from the church but from responsible participation in political and service organizations which they once believed could make a difference. The despair of students on college, university, and schools of theology campuses is abundant evidence that they see no hope for their lives to make any difference. They feel there is no way to count in removing the injustices and making the changes required for life worth living. Their homes are polluted with suspicion and distrust and so is their city, nation, and world. There is no soul food, no meaning to live by!

In my thirty years as a pastor, I have been awakened many times at one or two in the morning by a cop-out from life who cries bitterly through his drunken stupor for some way to change the mess in his life and home and world. Recently I have talked with other cynical dropouts who have taken neither alcohol nor drugs. They have simply chosen the easiest and least costly approach to get all the pleasure and fun out of life in the *now,* for there is nothing sure to believe or to hold on to in the *future.*

There have been other crises of faith. Twenty-three civilizations have already perished "from loss of nerve," says Arnold Toynbee. One of these was the Greco-Roman civilization that failed, as historian Mommsen puts it, because "the world was growing old and not even Caesar could make it young again."

The loss of nerve meant then what it means today: from the poorest to the richest, from the weakest to the strongest, too many had lost faith in the old gods and values which for many generations had been sustained by loyal self-discipline. Pleasure and security for the moment ranked higher than self-sacrifice for any cause however noble. Even Seneca, the Stoic philosopher, was completely cynical. In order to save his own wealth and honor, he wrote the speeches for the sadistic, dissolute tyrant Nero, by which Nero tried to justify the murder of his mother, his half-brother and sister, and numerous other persons who stood in his way. Though his people hated him they preferred to save their wealth or their dole rather than to oppose the obvious evils and injustices of their time. No wonder when the disciplined Goths and Vandals swept down from the North, the effete Romans were no match for them.

This loss of nerve is described poignantly by the prophets of the Old Testament as they spoke to the people of Israel in exile in Babylon. These sad souls were crying in their cups, "Things are past hope. We will do as we like, and each of us will follow the promptings of his own . . . heart" (Jer. 18:12, NEB).

The parallel in our own times to these illustrations from the past is painfully clear. Many people today, even those who still cling to the forms of the Judeo-Christian faith, answer in near despair as did the Hebrew people when their leaders called out to them, "Sing to the Lord a new song; sing to the Lord, all the earth" (Ps. 96:1, RSV). "How shall we sing the Lord's song in a foreign land?" (Ps. 137:4, RSV).

This is the origin of the hopelessness that grips much of mankind today. How shall we sing the Lord's song, a new song of hope and joy, in an unfriendly and hostile land where "megatechnology," promising us life, has given us meaninglessness, and where almost everything is going wrong, including our own personal lives?

The world is asking us, if God is not dead where is he? The fact that this attitude of pessimism belongs not only to the intellectual elite of our day such as Lewis Mumford and Alvin Toffler but also to the common man in the shop, the street, and the home is indicated by a sign on the walls of a restaurant frequented by truckers on Highway 66: "If you can keep your head when everyone around you is losing his, then you don't understand the situation."

The situation is difficult to understand. But as I have said there have been other times of pessimism and despair, and the same possibilities exist now as then. Charles Dickens begins *A Tale of Two Cities* with these words:

> It was the best of times, it was the worst of times,
> it was the age of wisdom, it was the age of foolishness,
> it was the epoch of belief, it was the epoch of incredulity,
> it was the season of Light, it was the season of darkness,
> it was the spring of hope, it was the winter of despair.

Only a person with an authentic faith in God is likely to believe for long that with all the possibilities of suffering and destruction, "these are the best of times!" Recently a radio and television commentator declared that these are the most critical times in the last ten thousand years. He said that there is less regard for law in our complex society which needs intelligent laws and respect for them more than any other in history. We now have a scientific technology that can send men to the moon or to Mars, but it fails to provide the meaning and loving cooperation that makes life and peace possible.

Illustrations of this fact are all too plentiful. I am acquainted with a famous scientist, well known in the realms of math and physics, whose personal and home life is a tragic failure. He respects and obeys the laws of physics. He is indifferent and disobedient to the laws of human relationships. His son, hungry for the love of a father he never had, tried to kill him. His wife divorced him. He is eager to cooperate with the forces of physical harmony and power, but he is fragmented in his own personal and social life.

All right, what then are we to do? Give up in despair and join in the escape through drugs or alcohol and/or a mad scramble for more material things and pleasures that satisfy less and less? We could escape to the sanctuaries of our churches, sing nice, soft songs, listen to comforting messages that give us "peace of mind," and leave the mess up to God! But when we do, we soon find that all these means of escape have a way of turning life in on us and leaving us emptier than ever. I like the story of the large woman who stood on the scales without knowing they were out of order. The hand went only to seventy pounds. A little boy watching responded, "Whew! She's hollow!" What an appropriate description of so many of us and our "things" in this "new day!" As T. S. Eliot says so graphically:

> We are the hollow men
> We are the stuffed men
> Leaning together
> Headpiece filled with straw. Alas![7]

So the profound question is, how do we get "unstuffed" from all the clichés, negativisms, and self-denying, life-denying unfaiths? How do we fill our hollowness with a realistic faith[8] that leads us to creative, joyful living and action in this critical era?

Whether or not we join in the pessimism and escape or in the desperate methods of rebellious anarchy and the corresponding repression depends on the nature and depth of our faith. What is the ultimate word of reality? What is the mightiest force in the universe? This is not purely abstract or philosophical; it is a *life* question. Our answer to it will determine our hope and courage to act, or as Lewis Mumford puts it,

> For those of us who have thrown off the myth of the machine, the next move is ours: for the gates of our technocratic prison will open automatically, despite their rusty ancient hinges, as soon as we choose to walk out.[9]

This seems to be an oversimplification, but it is *true* in the very nature of things *if* there is that Source and Giver of life who is trustworthy and is working with us to open the doors when we fulfill the requirements. It is only then that we are likely to choose to "walk out"!

There are plenty of cynics who assert that there is no force capable of healing our divisions or of bringing understanding and cooperation into our polarized homes, campuses, nation, and world. They insist that nothing can enable us to work together as races and peoples. So they listen with utter skepticism to such optimistic calls as that of Colonel John Glenn at the beginning of the space age. As he returned to earth from that first momentous earth orbit, he said, "Let man take over."

The question is, how and when will man take over? And even more basic, do we believe that he really can? The whole concept of man depends on our belief in the nature of the universe of which man is but a part. The crisis is one of faith and there will be no new song worth singing until we meet it! If the mightiest forces in the universe today are the H-bombs, the rockets, the fire power of armies, the hatred of mobs, it is not likely that man will take over anything except a ruined pile of atomic dust or a despoiled world polluted and wrecked by our own gases and greeds!

But I believe that man can and will take over when he learns to respect, obey, and trust the mightiest force in the universe—Christlike, caring love, supremely revealed in Jesus. As Christians we know he is with us and is challenging us to join him in releasing this power.

The nature of this power is summed up in the hymn which Anita Bryant sang at the Super Bowl game on January 1, 1971.

In the beauty of the lilies Christ was born across the sea,
With a glory in his bosom that transfigures you and me;
As he died to make men holy [whole, complete, their fullest selves],
let us [live and] die to make men free! [free to love,
to sacrifice themselves for the good of all]
While God is marching on.
Glory! glory! Hallelujah! . . .
His truth is marching on.

What is this truth that is marching on? Impersonal, unconscious force? Integrating principle? What is the nature of this God, this deepest reality, who is marching on?

An inscription I found pinned on the door of the student senate office in one of our universities had this quote from D. H. Lawrence, "Heaven knows what we mean by Reality: telephones, tinned meat, Charlie Chaplin, water taps and world salvation, presumably!" I don't know about telephones and water taps, but I believe the highest Reality is concerned with personal and world salvation—salvation from the fears, hates, greeds, and terrors of man's inhumanity to the love that sets us free to life that is full and vital. Any other kind of freedom is empty!

Dag Hammarskjöld, great Swedish statesman and secretary general of the United Nations, believed that the man of Galilee best sums up the mighty truth that describes the awesome power ruling our universe. He was one of the thousands whose lives have been made meaningful and creative by their belief that through Jesus Christ comes the gift of meaning and hope for humanity. Writing in his diary on Christmas Eve, 1960, one year and a half before his tragic death in the Congo, Dag Hammarskjöld declared the faith to which his life was joined. "How proper it is that Christmas should follow Advent.—For him who looks towards the future, the Manger is situated on Golgotha, and the Cross has already been raised in Bethlehem."[10]

Gustaf Aulén, commenting on Dag Hammarskjöld's faith, says that for him "the whole life-achievement of Jesus is to be seen as an incarnation of the love of God—of God in man." And I would add the love of man for man because of this love of God. Hammarskjöld's life motto was in the last lines of an old Swedish hymn: ". . . there is nothing that is not won by the love which suffers."[11]

Is it true that the mightiest force on earth is the invincible power of the Spirit that was in Jesus and in the strong, humble, loving life to which he calls? Is it true that nothing is ever won but by the love that suffers?

I have believed this most of my life, and with conscious, understanding commitment since I was eighteen, but there have been moments of doubt. After making my decision in college to study for the Christian ministry because of this new found faith, I found myself faced with the convictions of intelligent men such as Henry Nelson Wieman, John Dewey, and others who claimed that the only God there is must be something like the group equivalent of Santa Claus or the sum total of values most important to man! They believed that prayer at its best is autosuggestion and self-hypnotism or just good positive thinking! This humanistic picture of man, who despite his longing for a loving Father-Creator must go it alone, left me in a major crisis. My emotional and mental stability was threatened, as well as my chosen ministry.

I was indeed on the verge of a crack-up, when one night I walked out along Turtle Creek in Dallas where I was finishing my studies in the Perkins School of Theology. I faced three alternatives: (1) go ahead and crack under the strain of the conflict of doubts unresolved; (2) be honest and quit trying to believe what I could not prove, get out of the ministry, and get all I could from life at the moment, doing good if it pleased me or forgetting it when it was more convenient; (3) learn and practice the faith that the persons I admired most claimed to have made all the difference in their lives. That night by an act of faith I decided to cast my lot with those whose faith in God as revealed and interpreted in Jesus had enabled them to make such large contributions to the betterment of mankind.

That act of faith brought me to a fresh burst of courage and hope and corresponding creativity. My personality and effectiveness grew and life was full. How I came to this act of faith and what it means to me now, I will describe later. Here let me simply affirm that I have continued to have doubts as I have seen again and again unscrupulous persons taking advantage of kind and loving people and as I have endured the horrors of living through World War II and other tragic events in these last forty years. At times I have rebelled until there was given me some fresh revealing of the deepest truth of life—that "nothing is ever won but by the love that suffers," for "love is of God and God is love."[12] I agree with Dostoyevsky that "My hosannas have gone through whirlwinds of doubt." Doubtless Dag Hammarskjöld and every other man or woman of faith would say the same thing. For surely he who has never doubted has never truly believed.

How can I be certain? This question points up the crisis of faith in this age of assurance and belief in the scientific world of physical achievements and of doubt and frustration in the personal and social world. It is right here that the ability to love and give oneself for others is so lacking and yet so necessary. The fact that so many are *unsure* or simply *do not believe* this basic assumption that strong, wise love is deep down at the heart of things is both our first problem and our greatest tragedy. For how can we be interested in God's will and his purpose for our lives unless there is at least this minimum conviction upon which we are willing to live and die? How else can we answer the questions, "Does might make right?" "Do hatred and selfishness really pay in the long run?" "Is sacrificial, self-giving love really foolish?"

Suppose I believe that my answer to these questions is simply my own choice and the opposite may be just as true for someone else—that is, self-giving love may be true for St. Francis and Albert Schweitzer, but whether or not I choose to give myself out of such love matters only to me. Then if there is no truth common to us all, how indeed could there be any respect for the laws of man that are based on "common good" when there is no common good? But we know the necessity of protecting the well-being of others from the freedom of the few to do as they please. Clearly, the morality upon which our human health and existence depend rests upon our faith or unfaith in the highest understanding of God we know: *Is or is not Christlike, caring love the mightiest force ruling the lives of man?* As Ivan in Dostoyevsky's novel *The Brothers Karamazov* put it, "Since there is no God and no devil, then everything is permissible," and he proceeded to justify the murder of his father. If anything goes, why be concerned about injustice in Vietnam or in our cities? Why respect the value of persons, if man is nothing but "a forked radish" with no destiny beyond a dusty death, "a vertical vertebrae with a perfect sewage system"? (Haeckel)

How do we know? How can we be sure enough to discover and

sing the new song for our new age in spite of the cacophony of noisy contradictions? In responding to these questions, it seems to me that there are four things required of each of us.

First, we must be *convinced* of the reality of God as seen most clearly in the spirit, life, death, and victory of Jesus Christ.

Second, we must be *reconciled* to the loving purposes of this Mighty Spirit who rules the universe but gives us freedom to fight and reject ourselves and our true destiny.

Third, we must be *committed* without reservations to live our lives in line with those purposes as we are able to discover and understand them.

Fourth, we must be *disciplined* voluntarily by continued acts of faith through the use of the means that best enable us to live and die by this faith.

NOTES

1. Lewis Mumford, *The Myth of the Machine—the Pentagon of Power* (New York: Harcourt, Brace Jovanovich, 1970), p. 57.

2. Ibid., pp. 73–74.

3. Ibid., p. 106.

4. Ibid., p. 186.

5. Alvin Toffler, *Future Shock* (New York: Random House, 1970), pp. 306–15.

6. Ibid., p. 353.

7. T. S. Eliot, "The Hollow Men," *Collected Poems 1909-1962*. Copyright, 1936, by Harcourt, Brace Jovanovich, Inc.; Copyright © 1963, 1964 by T. S. Eliot. Reprinted by permission of the publisher.

8. By the word *faith* I mean the convictions about those meanings and values we consider ultimate—what we are willing to stake our lives upon.

9. Mumford, p. 435.

10. Dag Hammarskjöld, *Markings* (New York: Alfred A. Knopf, 1964), p. 198.

11. Gustaf Aulén, *Dag Hammarskjöld's White Book* (Philadelphia: Fortress Press, 1969), p. 84.

12. Cf. 1 John 4:7–12.

2 What Faith Requires

How can secular, scientifically oriented man in the clutches of the new god megatechnology be *convinced* of the reality of a spiritually oriented universe ruled by the spirit of the One whose life has opened to us the wise love that orders and sustains all things?

First, I believe that such convincing may not be any more difficult now than it was for the skeptical secularists of the Apostle Paul's day who said the preaching of the cross is "a stumbling-block to Jews and folly to Greeks" (1 Cor. 1:23, NEB). Nor is it more difficult than in the first Age of Rationalism when God was either denied or pushed back into the beginnings with everything from rocks to man left to a chain of cause and effect. And yet it was in this eighteenth-century Age of Reason that the great awakening led by the Wesleys brought to hundreds of thousands the assurance of "Love Divine, All Loves Excelling."

The difference is that appearing in the most unexpected and unlikely places in two thousand years of Christian history, we have the evidences in the lives of men and women who have risen to Christlike heights of concern for their fellows. They began movements in which their influence was extended far beyond the number of followers whom they personally touched.

For example, what more unlikely time or situation than the second century when brutish persecutions left most of the Christian leaders and thousands of their followers either dead or broken in body and spirit? Only about one-tenth of the Christians in Southern France survived, and many of these had bought their lives by

27

leaving a pinch of salt in token worship before the statue of the emperor. Who could have foreseen that in such difficult times, Irenaeus, the brave young Bishop of Lyons, would have been the means by which there came a remarkable restoration of the vigor and influence of the Christian faith? Who would have guessed this renewal of faith was to bring new hope and vitality to human life during the decadence and fall of the once mighty Roman Empire? Yet the restoration did take place through a fresh understanding of the life, teachings, and victory of Jesus Christ whom Irenaeus described as *Christus Victor*. Irenaeus believed and taught that Jesus is the true human being who "agonized and conquered" because he represented the "one God and Father. . . . The one superior to suffering [is seen] becoming subject to suffering and the Word becoming man. Thus he sums up all things in himself."[1]

Christus Victor was made known to the discouraged and defeated Christians of that dark day by the presentation for the first time of the four Gospels for use in worship. Here the people heard the amazing apostolic witness to the victorious Christ who is still present wherever the people of God gather in his name—the human experience of the spirit of Jesus let loose in the world through the Holy Spirit. The same thing happened to them as happens today when young or old encounter the Christ. Through hearing the New Testament account of the life, death, and resurrection of Jesus, they were convinced that in him God had come very near to them. As these now courageous Christians met for worship, they knew that the Roman emperor did not have the last word. *The last word is with God in Christus Victor!*[2]

The Word read from the Gospels was interpreted and convincing through the Word seen in the life of Irenaeus and his followers. One of the first tasks, therefore, for anyone desiring to find the new song for this dangerous but challenging age is to become familiar with the lives and writings of men and women of the past and present who have made the Word from the New Testament come alive in their own indomitable faith.

Listen to the very personal evidence from another early Christian, Cyprian of Carthage, about A.D. 250. As you do, you can begin to understand how through every century there have been those whose lives of faith and joy resulted in responsible love for their fellows. They were contagiously convincing to countless others. From a garden in Carthage, Cyprian was writing to his friend Donatus during a period of relentless persecution within the shadow of the impending fall of the Roman Empire.

> This seems to be a cheerful world, Donatus, when I view it from this fair garden under the shadow of these vines. But if I climbed some great mountain and looked out over the wide lands you know very well what I would see. Brigands on the high roads, pirates on the seas, in the amphitheatres men murdered to please applauding crowds, under all roofs misery and selfishness. It is really a bad world, Donatus, an incredibly bad world. Yet in the midst of it I have found a quiet and holy people. They have discovered a joy which is a thousand times better than any pleasures of this sinful life. They are despised and persecuted, but they care not. They have overcome the world. These people, Donatus, are the Christians—and I am one of them.[3]

Since the time of Cyprian, the problems have become more complex and the evil more threatening because of the indescribably greater destructive powers available. But the way to meet our twentieth-century problems still depends on the convincing powers of faith in the lives of those who have found the reality of Christlike love ruling their actions and giving hope for the future.

One of the most convincing of all those whose life experiences have had positive influence on mankind is the story of St. Francis. Francis was the dissolute young son of Pietro, a rich merchant in the city of Assisi in thirteenth-century Italy. His brilliant and lovable personality made him the leader for the youth of his city. If he had ridden a motorcycle in our times, he would have made the most daring and audacious of "Hell's Angels." One night after a wild feast, as the gang rushed out into the streets to celebrate, they looked around to find Francis, the master of the revels for the night. But he had lagged behind them and for the second time in several days felt himself sick and empty in his petty and selfish life. He believed God was calling him to a new life of love for the sick and needy around him. When his companions found him and saw his face, they began to tease and accuse him of being "in love." How else could they explain his strange behavior!

"Yes," said Francis, "I am in love with a bride nobler and richer and fairer than you have ever seen." Roaring with laughter his friends went on their boisterous way.

A few days later Francis met a leper in the road. He started to

"stubbornness." But he and his wife Catherine were sure that to believe in Jesus Christ meant to care for all who were poor and needy, not only spiritually but physically. Many of the social reforms in England and America during the next seventy years came about through the influence of William and Catherine Booth and their "Army" of loving servants.

To his followers he said often, "No one ever heard the gospel half-frozen or half-starved." He fed the hungry, helped the unemployed find jobs, cared for alcoholics and prostitutes, and worked for prison reform and better labor laws. He founded the parole system. Four of his leaders went to India to embrace the life of the outcastes. Their spirit and methods influenced Gandhi, who had just been released from prison. Their worship was inseparable from their work. The best tribute that could be paid to Booth was at his funeral when Queen Mary slipped into the back seat and heard a former prostitute say, with tears of gratitude, "He cared for the likes of us."[5]

Another life made luminous by faith in the love that is the strongest power in the world was that of a brilliant young German musician born in 1875. His influence has spanned two world wars and given a stream of hungry persons meaning and hope for a life that counts. His name was Albert Schweitzer and he became the great Christian doctor of the Lambarene in Africa. His life started out inauspiciously. He was almost a failure in his music classes. Instead of practicing, he was too often improvising his own music. His teacher called him his "thorn in the flesh." In confirmation classes his brilliant, inquisitive mind asked questions the pastor couldn't answer. So Albert became afraid to ask his questions. Instead he memorized the proper answers and was confirmed, though the pastor warned that the lad would not amount to anything. "He is indifferent to matters of faith." But this young man became one of the greatest New Testament scholars of all times, an organist, and a world-renown interpreter of Bach. Then at the age of thirty, having attained the highest honors in music and theology, he surrendered his comfortable position to study medicine and then to go to the Lambarene as a doctor!

What had happened? Two things. In writing *The Quest of the Historical Jesus* he had found more than a task of textual criticism. He had met one who was to lead and challenge him to the end of his days. The other event was a chance discovery—or was it providence? On his desk at the theological college he picked up a green-covered magazine, the report of the Paris Missionary Society. He was absorbed by the description of how the French Congo was starved for workers. He closed the magazine and began his work. He knew his search was over. This was to be his "direct service" to pay back part of what God and his family and others had given to him so prodigally. His friends were astonished, then disgusted as he refused to heed such arguments as, "The Negro of Central Africa isn't your job. . . . Other men can work among the Africans, men without your gifts for scholarship and for art." He knew this was true, and yet there were not enough helpers going to meet the need which was so great. And so he went.

Why and how did he do it? Let him answer in the great words that describe the compulsions of Christlike love and the mystery of Jesus who first makes this love known. Before he left Africa he finished the book, *The Quest of the Historical Jesus*. The last paragraph in the last chapter gives his personal witness. Many reading it and knowing something of the author have been moved to a life of faith that also led to a life of self-giving love.

> As one unknown and nameless He comes to us, just as on the shore of the lake He approached those men who knew not who He was. His words are the same: "Follow thou Me!" and He puts us to the task, which He has to carry out in our age. He commands. And to those who obey, be they wise or simple, He will reveal Himself through all they are privileged to experience in His fellowship of peace and activity, of struggle and suffering, till they come to know, as an inexpressible secret, who He is.[6]

These are some of the many persons in every age, unknown and well known, whose life witness has convinced thousands of others. This convincing comes to those of us who are open to see evidence in human life, "signals of transcendence" as Peter Berger, Christian sociologist, calls them in his book *A Rumor of Angels*—the Christ Spirit changing, transforming, making caring love possible in persons, homes, groups, and whole societies. With all the brutalities of our age, the world *is* learning compassion. In spite of its evils and injustices, our day is much different from fifty years ago. And compare

our day with the setting a hundred or even a thousand years ago.
The difference can be seen in the widespread revulsion to indiscrim-
inate killing in Vietnam, a revulsion which did not occur even in
World War II or during the war in Korea, though the senseless
murder of innocent children and civilians as well as young men in
military service and the saturation bombing of both of these wars
were just as tragic. There is today in our world, and especially
among youth, an awareness of the value of persons that did not
exist even ten years ago. Yes, we have a long way to go, but we
have come a long way! I believe this journey could not have been
made without the influence of Christlike loving persons who found
their ideals and strength to love from their convictions of faith in
the love of Christ beneath and within and through all things.

Perhaps the most important of all evidences that may convince
of the reality of the Christlike loving spirit ruling the universe is
the evidence in the lives of vital Christians around us whom we
know personally. While it is true that actions do not always measure
up to intentions, I believe there is ample evidence in any community
and in any church of people whose commitment to Christ can be
clearly seen in their life styles.

My own convincing began with my parents' faith, which while
I rejected for a time, I could never question the fact that their
lives were different and admirable because of it. Since then I have
known many people who have lived the life of Christlike, self-
giving love so realistically and beautifully that I have been *convinced* as I came to know and share with them. They have proved
what Martin Luther called the greatest evidence of the love of God—
the possibility of ordinary men and women being "little Christs to
their neighbors."

The fact that Malcom X, as he reports in his autobiography,
never met such a vital Christian, white or black, until after he had
been in prison, represents one of the great tragedies of our time.
Though he lived in Lansing and Detroit, in Michigan, Boston, and
New York, where there were many such vital Christians, he never
knew one personally until he had already begun the Black Muslim
movement which was founded on hatred for white people. It was
only during and after his pilgrimage to Mecca that he met white
persons who had a recognizable love and concern for blacks. The
simple but tragic fact is that millions like him in our country and

around the world have never seen the power of love that conquers hate. No wonder we cannot bridge the gaps in our homes or those between races and peoples.

It is the love of Christ in the Apostle Paul, in Irenaeus, Cyprian, St. Francis of Assisi, John Wesley, William Booth, Frank Laubach, Albert Schweitzer, and in my mother and father and other committed Christians that has convinced me as it has countless others. Like these whom I have described, once we are convinced, we will be convincing in the authenticity of the joy, love, and hope of our own lives—*if* we go the remainder of the way.

RECONCILIATION

We can now take the next step in finding the new song for our own lives and age. As we are convinced by the reality we have discovered in Christ, a relationship results through which we are *reconciled to God, to ourselves, and then to our brothers.*

The meaning of this desperately needed reconciliation with Christ and thus with ourselves and our brothers may be summed up in four simple but crucial sentences. We need to be reconciled to God in respect to our *sin*, seeking to save our false pictures of life by *forgiveness*. We need to be reconciled to God in respect to his *requirements*—the given in which we live—by *obedience*. We need reconciliation to God in respect to his *appointments*—the frailty and freedom of our human situation—by *trust*. And we need reconciliation to God in respect to the *new relations to other persons in brotherly love* which goes out to all men.

Unfortunately, the word *reconciliation* elicits a negative reaction from many people today, including many professing Christians. They can understand alienation and see its evil results. But because of their fears of other persons and groups, many believe that attempts at reconciliation are selling out and therefore signs of weakness rather than strength. For them the only solution to alienation is to persuade or force the other to capitulate. Mankind has so often mistaken *reconciliation* for *compromise*; but there is another and more creative approach which the Apostle Paul offers. "God was in Christ reconciling the world to himself, . . . and entrusting to us the message of reconciliation" (2 Cor. 5:19, RSV).

Perhaps the paraphrase of these words by Clarence Jordan in

The Cotton Patch Version of Paul's Epistles may shed light on their meaning.

> This is God's doing all the way through. It is he who, through Christ, bridged the gap between himself and us and who has given us the job of also bridging the gap. God was in Christ, hugging the world to himself . . . and has planted in us his concern for getting together. So now we represent Christ and it is as though God were pleading through us. In Christ's behalf we urge you to open up to God.

Obviously the figure of speech, *hugging the world to himself,* could be written off as sentimental rubbish, but it is really a significant symbol that represents the heart of reconciling love.

Here is a rather personal illustration of what I believe is meant. When as a boy of six I made fun of my little sister and brother, they hit me and I hit them back and all of us were crying. My mother waded in and gave me a few well-directed spanks that hurt my ego more than my bottom. There were tears in her eyes, and I wondered why. I hadn't hurt her. Or had I? She then took me on her lap and hugged me and told me she forgave me because God had. She told me that in hurting Jewel and John, I had hurt myself *and* her *and* God. That was news to me! Then she turned to my brother and sister, "Jewel and John, do you forgive Lance?" And then to me, "Lance, do you forgive Jewel and John?" This question was important to me, for even though I had started the battle, I was bitter and resentful toward Jewel and John who had in turn hurt me. Each of us nodded our affirmative answer. Mother hugged me again, kissed me, and when I got down from her lap, I was free to love and to play with Jewel and John as though nothing had happened! We were reconciled through our mother's love to God, to each other, and to ourselves.

To be reconciled to God in *respect to sin with forgiveness* does not mean that the wrong doesn't matter. Sin hurts very much; but because of the love coming from God, we are forgiven, free to begin again, free to love and work and play together as we could not before. This is the forgiveness of reconciliation that every family, every church and community, all the people of the world need. It comes as it is mediated through other human beings who live out the love of Christ! And this is something to sing about: "They shall know we are Christians by our love."

Reconciliation to God in respect to his *requirements* resulting in *obedience*—how desperately this is needed by each of us and by our entire human race. The breakdown of civil law is a by-product of the breakdown of moral law. If there is no moral law except "my idea," "my way," or "your idea," "your truth," there is nothing to command respect. No wonder there is chaos in morality when the foundations of faith in the requirements for human life are crumbling.

For thirty years I have counseled couples whose homes were breaking up over the obvious demands of each party that the other go "my way or else!" The *else* was always further alienation and hostility and, in the end, hatred and divorce. I have never yet seen a failing marriage become a successful one as long as both husband and wife said, "I must have things my way—I must be free to do as I please—I can't stand quarrels, I had enough quarreling between my parents as a child." True harmony and unity come even in the diversity of two separate individuals only when there is a common allegiance to a higher authority than themselves—when both the man and the woman are open to the third viewpoint, the truth of God's way, the requirements built into the very nature of human life. The morality of respect and concern for each other is rooted in a faith that they are both under a higher law than their own demands.

I recall dozens of couples that could never have made it on the old basis of "my way" versus "your way" who have established a family relationship that is a little island of security, belonging, and reconciliation. It all began to happen when they genuinely began to pray with all their hearts, "Our Father, your will be done . . . your requirements for our home and our lives be fulfilled." The requirements for life go far beyond hedonistic pleasure or the egoistic will to power. Only those who earnestly seek for and obey these requirements ever find life that has harmony and joy in it.

A great many stories have arisen out of the terrible times of testing in the hunger and suffering of our age of war and the various political tyrannies that have robbed countless millions of freedom and life. I recommend three true accounts of such experiences to anyone who thinks that the morality of love and respect for others and for oneself so desperately needed in our machine age is likely or even possible without some strong conviction, some higher faith in the ultimate concern of the Creator-Spirit for all mankind.

In his book *From Death-Camp to Existentialism*, Dr. Viktor E. Frankl makes plain the deep conviction by which he came through the horrible fears and privation of the concentration camps. As far as he could tell, he says, no one survived without a strong faith that there is some ultimate meaning beneath all things, even the worst evils. "When one has a 'why' he can stand any kind of 'how!' " Without faith in Ultimate Meanings, he writes, there can be no reason or resource within human life for moral living, or in some situations for any living at all.

Langdon Gilkey, now professor at the University of Chicago, describes his experiences in *Shantung Compound* where he was a prisoner of the Chinese Communists along with several hundred Americans, British, Dutch, and Germans. He tells how quickly the shell of conventional morality fell from most of the inmates. They would lie, cheat, steal, and hurt each other in order to get another bit of food or comfort. Self-preservation on the animal level seemed to be the law of life for most of them. He witnessed the utter breakdown of morality, that is, any genuine concern for others, any willingness to sacrifice.

The breakdown occurred, strangely enough, in two opposite kinds of persons: (1) in those who professed no faith or allegiance to anything or anyone higher than their own self-interest and preservation, and (2) in those who in the beginning were most vocal in professing their Christian faith. These latter were the literalists and legalists whose faith was based on the rigid authoritarian theology that said in effect, "The Lord cares for his own—when you are righteous you will not suffer—when you suffer you are not righteous." They were righteous, therefore this was unfair, unjust. They were among the meanest and most insensitive to the needs of others, though their professions of the Christian faith were the loudest. A few who did not openly profess any faith showed faith in a moral concern that put to shame these "professional Christians." Langdon Gilkey, seeing this breakdown in morality by both groups, went through the agonizing experience of losing what faith he had. Then he began to realize that the only ones who remained moral, that is, were able to care for their fellows and were willing to sacrifice themselves for those in great need, were the ones who possessed a deep conviction —a faith, whether articulated or not, that the deepest and highest reality behind and beneath all existence is connected with the value of persons.

The third account makes even more explicit this relationship between the morality of loving concern for others and faith in God whose love is utterly dependable. It is the story of Ernest Gordon, university-trained commander of the 93rd Highlanders from Scotland, who was a prisoner of the Japanese in the POW Camp by the River Kwai in Thailand during World War II. He describes the deteriorating conditions as the prisoners, starved and overworked, were stricken by cholera and other diseases. In the previous camp the old patterns of army life sustained them. "We had still shown some consideration for one another. Now that was gone, swept away. Existence had become so miserable, the odds so heavy against us, that nothing mattered except to survive. We lived by the rule of the jungle, 'red in tooth and claw' the evolutionary law of the survival of the fittest. It was a case of 'I look out for myself and to hell with everyone else.' . . . The weak were trampled underfoot, the sick ignored or resented, the dead forgotten. When a man lay dying we had no word of mercy. When he cried for our help, we averted our heads. . . . Everyone was his own keeper. . . . It was free enterprise at its worst, with all the restraints of morality gone. . . . Little acts of meanness, suspicion, and favoritism permeated our daily lives. . . . It was a common practice to steal from one another. . . .

"We had no church, no chaplains, no services. If there were men who kept faith alive in their hearts they gave no sign. This was not surprising. At Changi many had turned to religion as a crutch. But the crutch had not supported them; so they had thrown it away. Many had prayed, but only for themselves. Nothing happened. They had sought personal miracles from the Bible and none had come. They had appealed to God as an expedient. But God apparently had refused to be treated as one.

"We had long since resigned ourselves to being derelicts. We were forsaken men—forsaken by our families, by our friends, by our government. Now even God had left us.

"Hate, for some, was the only motivation for living. We hated the Japanese. We would willingly have torn them limb from limb, flesh from flesh, had they fallen into our hands. In time even hate died, giving way to numb, black despair."[7]

Then the miracles of the spirit of love and concern began to happen. Gordon himself was stricken and spent horrible days in the "Death House," but was rescued by a friend who introduced him to two young soldiers, Dinty and Dusty. One was a Methodist; the other, a Roman Catholic. Both lived their faith without talking about it in an obtrusive way. They took it upon themselves to nurse him night and day. They washed his gangrenous legs, massaged his body, and "mucked" for him (that is, shared their own meager food, sacrificing what they needed to keep him alive and then to help him get well).

Gordon was bitter and unbelieving, but Dusty and Dinty kept him informed of the strange miracle taking place in the camp through the remarkable sacrifice of several men who had given their lives for their comrades. One whose name was Angus had mucked for his sick friend, giving him his blanket in the cold and the little food he had, until he himself died of exhaustion. Another Argyll saved his whole company one evening when the Japanese guards counted the tools with which they had been working and found one shovel missing. They accused the men of stealing it to swap with the Thais for food. Screaming curses, one of the guards raised his rifle, "All die, all die." Then the Argyll stepped forward saying, "I did it." The guard struck him in the head with his rifle, kicking and cursing him until he was dead.

These two stories added to several more accounts such as that of Dusty and Dinty began to change the attitude of most in the camp. A new concern for each other began to emerge. Officers and men began to share of their little with the sick.

Gordon was mystified. He knew Dusty and Dinty had something that made them concerned about him as he would not have been concerned about another person. He began to discuss his doubts and they began to share their faith.

"We may dream about love, truth, beauty and aspiration for our own amusement to dull the ache of our existence," Gordon reminded Dusty. "In fact, it's about all we can do. Actually, they're nothing but froth on the way. . . . Religion and the arts . . . help numb the senses. But drugs can do that much better."

Dusty was puzzled but affirmed his faith as he answered, with spirit, "No sir, I cannot believe that. I don't think there IS anything accidental about our creation. God knows us. . . . We cannot see everything He is doing now. . . . We have to go on living and hoping, having faith that life is stronger than death. Only God can give life. We have to receive it and that daily."

Then Dinty spoke his contribution, sharing the wisdom of his own faith. "Remember the old saying at home? 'We are a' Jock Tamson's bairns and we've a' got to hang together.' "

"And what's that supposed to mean?" Gordon asked skeptically.

"Well you might say it means—wait a minute—hmm—you might say it means—that we are all God's children and we've got to stick together. How's that?"

Ernest Gordon agreed it was very good. "True there was hatred," he wrote, "but there was also love. There was death, but there was also life. God had not left us. He was with us, calling us to live the divine life in fellowship. I was beginning to feel the miracle that God was working in the Death Camp by the River Kwai."[8]

His conclusion emphasizes the necessity to be reconciled to God in respect to his requirements through obedience. "Death was still with us—no doubt about that. But we were being slowly freed from its destructive grip. We were seeing for ourselves the sharp contradiction between the forces that make for life and those that make for death. Selfishness, hatred, jealousy and greed were anti-life. Love, self-sacrifice, mercy and creative faith, on the other hand, were the essence of life, turning mere existence into living in its truest sense. These were the gifts of God to men."[9]

Little wonder that when Ernest Gordon returned home he made the sharing of his new found faith the center of his life and concern. He is now the chaplain of Princeton University doing his bit not only to abolish war but the attitudes in man that cause war.

Now, we have no trouble respecting the laws in the physical universe. We may know they are relative to some extent, but they are so dependable we send our men to the moon and back and we travel by jet and motor car without questioning their dependability. We would not think of breaking these physical laws without the knowledge that we too would be broken. Astronaut Frank Borman, in his spaceship orbiting the moon, sent a message back to earth on Christmas, 1968, saying, "If we didn't know and obey God's physical laws in respect to our journey, we would not get home.

If you on that little green spaceship called earth do not discover and obey the moral and spiritual laws of your universe, we won't have any home."

Yet I sat at lunch one day with a young militant who boasted proudly of his freedom to destroy anything he desired, depending on what *"my* conscience says." He was at one with Robespierre and the other atheists of the French Revolution who in the name of their principles, "liberty, fraternity and equality," guillotined two hundred fifty thousand Frenchmen in a reign of terror scarcely equaled in human history! The truth is that when we lose the spirit of Christlike love as a motivating force, we are not enthusiastic over the requirements of life which Jesus summed up in the law of self-giving love for our neighbor. Why sacrifice for my neighbor if *I* am the supreme source of all that is good and worthy? I will be most unlikely to love my neighbor unless I believe I am loved and accepted by One who holds all of us within the greatness of his loving concern.

The third aspect of reconciliation with God may be even more difficult, but if so, it is equally important. Here I am required to be reconciled to him in respect to circumstances with a trust that includes many things I don't like and cannot understand and probably never will, at least in this life. We are born too tall or too short or with a weak constitution or a crippled body and many other conditions we can't change. I have often said that I was given for my own physical use a Volkswagen chassis and a Cadillac motor! If I could get by on five hours of sleep as some "great" persons do, there is no telling what I might accomplish! But I have to live with my need for seven or eight hours of sleep, with my Volkswagen chassis, physically speaking, and my Cadillac motor, mentally and emotionally speaking.

No wonder that at times we rebel against our human frailty, the circumstances of our birth, position, handicaps, opportunities or lack of them, and the final indignities of illness, pain, and death. What shall we do with our rebellion?

Let me share with you one of the many days in my own life when, by what I call the grace of God, I met my rebellion, self-pity, and resentment at my circumstances with the commitment of faith enabling me to trust.

On August 12, 1959, I was in a hotel room in Florence, Italy, critically sick with a perforated diverticulum and limited peritonitus. At least this was my doctor's diagnosis after I had described my symptoms by long-distance telephone. My wife Elizabeth and I were on a six-week tour of Europe. We had shared a good time in England and Scotland, in spite of some pain and the use of antibiotics which the doctor expected would get me well. But now while walking in Lucerne, Switzerland, the diverticulum had perforated. We had been to Milan and then to Venice where I really became so ill I could not get out of my room. There was no space on any plane returning to the United States so we went on to Florence, where I called my doctor and was able to get some more antibiotics. He told me to stay in bed and return to the United States as soon as possible—he could not operate until the infection was healed anyway. I had sent Elizabeth on to see the art treasures of Florence.

Alone in my room, I spent the first hour in self-pity and near despair. I thought I simply could not stand the noisy roar of the motor cars on the street three stories below. Their clamorous racket tore at my mind—symbolic of the fears that wrenched my very soul. Whether I had a cancer or would ever get home, or get well, I did not know. Then I said, with all the objectivity I could muster, "Lance Webb, you have been preaching to others the necessity to trust themselves to the love of God no matter their circumstances and then to make the most of them. Now, how about practicing what you preach? How about trusting?"

I did. That moment I submitted myself to God in my situation. Here are the words I used as I wrote them on that day's page in my inner life's notebook.[10] They communicate my response to God in that day's circumstances.

"O God, I accept whatever it is I must go through—a violent illness, yes, even if this must come—an operation—whatever—or if a time of rest and renewal—*O Lord, I accept the good in each minute*—

"O Lord, I love and accept this—this hour. I trust my present and future to you. Amen."

That hour I was set free! I was able to enjoy truly one of the most beautiful and fruitful days of my life! In my reading and thinking I found insights that were to grow and blossom in the years ahead. I was set free. I was whole and strong in spite of my seriously critical physical circumstances!

In the days ahead before complete recovery six months later, I had to repeat that act of trust many times, and in the months and years since. But this *one* thing I know: reconciliation by trust in the Eternal Love that will not let us go even in the worst circumstances is one of the most significant acts any human being can take.

Our ability to trust the Eternal Love in accepting the things we cannot change is symbolized by the story of a little boy standing with a famous botanist on the edge of a cliff. The botanist, seeing a rare and beautiful flower at the bottom of the ravine, offered to tie a rope around the waist of the little fellow and lower him down over the cliff, saying, "When you bring the flower back to me, I'll give you a dollar." The boy responded, "O.K., mister, it's a bargain. But first let me go get my father and let him hold onto the other end of the rope!"

The real question for man suspended over the abyss of frailty, evil, pain, and death is just this: "Who or what, if anything, has hold of the other end of the rope?" The frightening possibility is that the question may be answered, "No one." The moral irresponsibility, the escape through drugs, alcohol, materialism, hedonism, the surrender to the machine—all of these are in essence the by-products of the unfaith that convinces us there is no one at the other end of the rope!

With this uncertainty as to the ultimate meaning and destiny of human life, it is little wonder that so few of us are able creatively and helpfully to love our fellow-man. But when we believe reality is in some sure way like the Father of our Lord Jesus Christ and that he has hold of the other end of the rope, then "we are more than conquerors through him who loved us." Therefore nothing—nothing at all—"can separate us and the love of God in Christ" (paraphrase of Rom. 8:35–39).

Only in this state of inner freedom and security is it possible or likely that we will be able to be courageous and wise, to love even as we are loved! We can build bridges over the gaps caused by hostility, hate, greed, and prejudice by a realistic love that does the positive, creative, best things even in the worst times.

The fact that this bridge building is actually going on today in many places all over the world through the reconciling love of God in Christ is one of the most hopeful facts I know. In February,

1970, I returned from six weeks' visitation in Africa—the Congo, Rhodesia, Mozambique, and South Africa—with as great excitement as I have known. I had read the statement of one who knows present-day Africa to the effect that Africa is the *only* one of the continents today where Christianity is growing faster in numbers and influence —5 to 10 percent in all of Africa below the Sahara—than the growth in population!

After visiting numerous mission schools and hospitals, I still did not understand this phenomenon. It was only after dinner with two great Congolese chiefs, Shungu Koi near Wembo Nyama in the Central Congo and Myant Yav in Katanga, the richest province in the world, that I began to comprehend the situation. Both of these chiefs are active Christians, lay leaders in their two conferences of the church presided over by a Congolese bishop, John Wesley Shungu. We were talking about the rapid development of the Congo and the civil wars that had been so disastrous in slowing the development of their nation. I asked them what they considered the greatest needs of their people. In effect both of them gave the same answer.

"Yes, we need technological development, education in science and technics that will enable us to develop our unlimited physical resources. But first we need to help our people find the ability to love and work together in mutual cooperation, to be honest and dependable. Such unselfish love for each other is the only way to stop the curse of tribalism which brought about our civil war and the Biafran conflict and that causes the racism and wars between other peoples that could destroy the world. This can be done only through faith in Christ as we have come to know the meaning of God, the Father of all mankind."

These were handsome men, well educated, with a deep concern for their people. Chief Myant Yav is the former David Tshombe, brother of Moise Tshombe who had died in exile in Libya just a few months before. David had assumed the role of chief after his brother's tragic death, though to do so he had to surrender his lucrative mercantile business and assume a terrific burden of responsibility. His three-million Arund tribe is the largest in all Africa. Knowing that he and his family had suffered greatly, I was interested to know what he felt about President Mobutu and the possibilities for peace in the Congo. He answered frankly but with deep feeling,

"I hold nothing but forgiveness in my heart toward anyone. I am willing to cooperate with President Mobutu and to work together that we may have the opportunity to educate our people and to live at peace as God intended his family on earth to live." Knowing the background of such a statement, it is impossible for me to regard it other than a miracle of the reconciling love of Christ, not only in principle but in realistic practice. I sat at the table with this noble African chief knowing that in him and hundreds of others like him is the hope not only of the Congo, but of all Africa and of the world. He and his fellow believers are indeed *possessed* by a *realistic love* that does the *positive, creative, best things even in the worst times.*

Why is the number and influence of Christians growing in Africa? The answer was clear to me as I sat with these two noble men. The kind of Christians they had known were mostly those possessed by self-giving love—Christian doctors and teachers and pastors who had risked all in order to share their faith. They knew and lived the reconciling love of Christ through forgiveness, obedience, trust, and love! This is indeed something to sing about!

But *how* can we sing a new song for this new age with such old symbols to represent the meaning of this Reality?[11] Recently I was speaking to a group on this theme. In order to illustrate and express the new song, I had them sing the old spiritual, "He's Got the Whole World in His Hands." This is a very graphic description of the all-inclusive love that rules all things. When I had concluded the address, a woman came up to me, her eyes blazing with hostility. "You had me with you," she cried, "until you led us in singing that silly song, 'He's Got the Whole World in His Hands.' What final nonsense is this—this blasphemy?"

I had previously quoted the words of Bliss Carman: "Love is the great law that binds the world together safe and whole."[11] Now she threw the words back at me. "Love the final law in a broken, hopeless world? 'He's got the whole world in his hands!'—this God of love? Ha—how could this love you talk about let seventy thousand Peruvians slip through his fingers in a single earthquake? Or let the innocent suffer with the guilty in Vietnam, the Middle East, and Los Angeles? There is no higher law than the survival of the fittest! Love that is supposed to have the whole world in its hands is a mockery or a monster—it is not what I call 'love'!"

In that moment I looked at her. Realizing the background from which she came—a hard, self-righteous, legalistic father had taught her the wrath of a God she despised and had given her pat answers about the love of God in relation to such evils as earthquakes and human meanness—I could not answer in words that would remove her doubt and bitterness. Nor can I now speak some magic words that will do likewise for you who may hold the same rebellion she had. I did say to her as I do to you that, if you are open, God in Christ will answer your rebellion. "The Word [the intention of the Creator-Spirit] made flesh" so long ago in the human Jesus is coming today and will come tomorrow with hope and healing and a love that never lets go.

"Not one of these little ones shall perish," is the way Jesus said it, "so set your troubled hearts at rest! If you have known me, you have known my Father also."

Like Job, however, you and I cannot understand his ways; but we may cry with Job, "I know that my Redeemer lives" (Job 19:25, RSV). Unlike Job, we have the Word at Bethlehem and on the cross, the Word of forgiveness, of trust, of caring love! We have the risen Lord who in human life has conquered sin and pain and death and will "put all enemies under his feet" (1 Cor. 15:25, NEB). In human betrayal, in pain, in loss beyond compare, I know the *final* word is his, and I can wait for more understanding. And while I wait, I will open the door to love so that his light will shine into the dark where my brothers shiver, hurt, and die. I believe, with a faith that has been tried countless times, that he *has* the whole world in his hands and those hands will *never, never let go!*

COMMITMENT

When you and I come to such a convincing and reconciling relationship to this love that never lets go, we are ready to make a *commitment, a decision to live and act wholeheartedly by our faith.* Obviously, it is still a faith—that is, we do not *see* it *all.* We have no absolute proof. But we have to *choose* one way or another. Others have experienced such convincing, reconciling love, and when they were committed to live by their faith, they found through their own experience that such commitment leads to life that is creative, redemptive, and whole.

Nevertheless, for us as for them, *commitment is at the heart of*

faith—a decision to act without proof—for there is no absolute
convincing proof conclusive enough for the mind of a scientifically
oriented secular man or woman to accept. For instance, though I
shared with the woman mentioned earlier arguments for the reality
of the Love that has the world in its hands and will never let go,
my evidence was not sufficient. She demanded proofs which are not
there. Yes, there are plenty of evidences, but for some, the evidences
of experience may be very much on the other side of the coin as this
woman pointed out. Nevertheless, a choice must be made with all
the evidence we can find, a choice by faith that leads to action;
and the action is the best test, the best evidence of the validity of
our faith. "Jesus, well aware that the Father had entrusted everything
to him, and that he had come from God and was going back to
God, rose from table, laid aside his garments, and taking a towel,
tied it round him. Then he poured water into a basin, and began
to wash his disciples' feet and to wipe them with the towel" (John
13:3–5, NEB).

As a child Jesus was convinced of the strong, wise love of the
eternal Father. His struggles in the wilderness and in Gethsemane
indicate that he too had to be reconciled to the Father in meeting
the expectations of his people and his human desire to be saved
from suffering, sorrow, and death. He could say "The Father and
I are one" only by a supreme act of faith which was consummated
on Calvary. He answered his own question, "My God why? why hast
thou forsaken me?", with the commitment of faith, "Father, into
thy hands I commit my spirit."

"Jesus knowing that the Father had entrusted all things into his
hands"—this is indeed an act of faith. This is the key to his song
in the night of forsakenness and despair in Gethsemane—the acceptance of life as a sacred trust from God. And the final endowment
of all by God is the freedom to accept and respect the trust, to accept
life with humility, and to use it for the good of all my brothers and
sisters in the family of God, or to reject the trust, to throw life
away in stupid and vain self-seeking. One thing is sure, *we are
given the freedom to create or to destroy.* Yes, Mr. Mumford, man
can take over, as he is called to do. but only when by faith he
accepts the trust and acts responsibly in the spirit and according to
the purposes of his Creator-Father, Redeemer as revealed in the
Christ-Spirit in Jesus and in men and women of all ages.

There is an old legend apropos to our day. An aged wise man, beloved by most of the people in his village for his compassion, kindness, and wisdom, was envied by the village bully who determined to show the villagers what a fool the old man really was. The young man caught a live bird and called all the villagers to assemble in the square. "I'll show the old man how foolish he is. I will ask him if the bird is alive or dead. If he says the bird is alive, I will crush the bird. If he says the bird is dead, I will open my hands and let the bird go free. Either way you will see that the old man is a fool." So with the villagers all assembled, the young man asked the old sage, "I have a bird in my hand. Is it alive or is it dead?" The old man answered quietly, "As you will, my son, as you will!"

So the sacred trust of the mightiest power in the universe is ours. We have been entrusted not only with the power of the H-bomb, rockets, jet planes, laser beams, and automated machines, but also with the power to accept our amazing lives and all this breathtaking physical power. Why? The answer of faith declares that it is not for ourselves alone. It is to be lived and used in loving humility as we work with our fellows in bringing justice and peace to our homes, our society, and our world! The question requires an act of faith. What will you do with this power, this sacred trust? "As *you* will, my son, as you *will!"*

Surely the greatest spirits of every age who have contributed their lives and works to the well-being of human life have been the ones who by faith have sung the new song for their age. They have joined with the ancient singer of the Hebrews in exile who committed himself to the meaning and purposes of God. "I *will* sing to the Lord as long as I live; I *will* sing praise to my God while I have being" (Ps. 104:33, RSV, italics mine).

One of the most inspiring examples of the commitment of faith I have seen among the youth of our day is the story of the way two young people are meeting the tragedies resulting from the war in Vietnam. I know of many others—some who chose the way of conscientious objectors and courageously paid the price, others who lost their loved ones but who refused to be bitter. This young man chose to keep his commitment as a member of the air force in Vietnam where he served as one of the crew of a helicopter. I heard the story from the lips of his wife, a lovely hostess on an Ozark

Airlines plane. My wife and I were flying from Indianapolis to Springfield when I noticed this young woman's joy and excitement. I asked her why she seemed so happy.

"Because tomorrow is my last day with Ozark!"

"Oh, don't you like flying?"

"Yes, indeed, and Ozark is one of the best companies for which to work; but Wednesday, Jimmy is coming home!"

Her eyes sparkled as she told their story. Jimmy had been in Vietnam for nearly a year when his helicopter was shot down. All of the crew were killed except him, and his leg was so badly wounded that later it was amputated at the hip. For several days he was missing, and some friendly Vietnamese cared for him in an obscure village in the South. Here, in great pain and loneliness, he met a little Vietnamese girl about five years old whose family had been killed in the war. When he was finally found and brought to the hospital, he had become so attached to the little girl that he took her with him. The medics at the hospital found ways to provide for her while Jimmy was getting well. He had written Joyce about her, and Joyce immediately sent her some clothes and a pair of shoes.

Joyce enlisted the aid of her church group and collected enough money to buy shoes for other Vietnamese children. When she took the money she had saved to buy postage, she was told the government would send the shoes postage paid. So she used the money to buy more shoes. Then came a letter from Jimmy saying he was returning home and wanted to bring the little girl and adopt her as their daughter. This he was doing with Joyce's happy permission. And now excitedly she awaited his return and the beginning of a new life with a husband trying to walk on one good leg and an artificial one and with a new Vietnamese daughter.

I knew there was more to the story, so I asked how she could be so happy when their lives had withstood such injustices? Was Jimmy bitter about his experiences? No, Jimmy was not bitter. He had no hatred toward the Vietnamese, but thought they were a loving and attractive people. Yes, he believed it a tragedy that so many thousands should pay such a price for the selfishness and mistrust of people of the world. He had accepted his handicap with thanksgiving that he still had his life and one good leg. They were both praying for the war to end and would do anything to help get it over. Others had paid a greater price than they for this human folly, and they had each other and their new little adopted daughter.

How did she and Jimmy come to such a loving, positive approach to their difficulties? Here, she spoke quietly of two loving families in which both were brought up, of their church where they had been taught that life with all its evils and tragedies is good if the meanings and purposes of the Heavenly Father were sought and accepted. It was a simple faith, but as I look back on our conversation and can now visualize the kind of home this young couple will be making for the little victim of the insanity of the war in Vietnam, I know I was seeing another miracle of human life. Here was the harmony and love which come as the fruit of commitment to live by faith in the Eternal Love that never, never lets us go. When I contrast this with the bitterness and despair of many others I know, including some who professed the Christian faith, I know there is a difference. Some have found the new song for our new age; others have not. I know now as then that the heart of the song is the "great I will." I will commit my life to trust and obey the highest Reality I can think of—the Reality of the loving truth seen in the human Jesus and in his risen Spirit in the lives of those who accept themselves as members of God's family on earth.

DISCIPLINE

We are all interested in fruits such as these I have described. But *who cares about the roots?* This is really the heart of our problem. Every person, anywhere, is interested in life in the Age of Aquarius, but who is really interested in *disciplines?* Indeed it seems to be another bad word.

When I mentioned to my two daughters and their husbands (all under thirty) the title I had chosen for this book, they warmed immediately to the last part concerning the Age of Aquarius. Though they do not go for astrology, that is, very much, they agreed with me that most people today would come nearer knowing what I meant if I called our age, the Age of Aquarius, than if I spoke of it in biblical terms such as the "age when the Kingdom of Heaven is here." People will certainly turn you off if you begin talking in these terms, they assured me. What do most people know or care about the Kingdom of Heaven? But they rebuked me for daring

to use the word *disciplines* even coupled with such an "in" word
as *Aquarius*. Youth and most older folk, they told me, are simply
not interested in disciplines. Everyone wants to do his own thing.

So I was ready to give in and change to "Style of Life" or "Requirements for Life," when I began to talk with members of the
generation just younger than my own children. I was surprised to
discover how open the generation five to ten years younger are to
the words *disciplines, methods,* or *ways* by which order and meaning, harmony and joy may be found in life. Consider the number
of communes and other disciplined groups who are living and acting
according to certain mutually adopted principles or disciplines or
styles—call them what you will. Obviously, most youth and adults
are still undisciplined but they want something worth disciplining
themselves for!

The key is whether or not we have found that *something*—the
values and goals worthy of the most ardent and enthusiastic self
and group disciplines.

Of course, if this is really the twilight of humanity's hopes and
dreams, the tragic ending of the Age of Pisces, as the astrologers
describe the waning days of the old age when we as human beings
with our megatechnology combined with our hatred and fear of
each other may very well fight and destroy each other, then no one
is interested in anything remotely resembling discipline. Then "doing
my thing while I can" is only sensible!

Many young people and others who have seen the hopelessness of
depending principally on science and megatechnology are saying that
we may indeed be experiencing the birth pangs of a new age which
they are calling, in the language of astrology, the Age of Aquarius!
One of the most popular songs at this writing comes from the Broad-
way musical *Hair*. The song "Aquarius" describes in secular terms
almost exactly what the New Testament calls the Kingdom of Heaven
on earth (that is, excluding the astrological introduction).

> When the moon is in the seventh house
> and Jupiter aligns with Mars,
> Then peace will guide the planets,
> And love will steer the stars;
> This is the dawning of the age of Aquarius. . . .
> Harmony and understanding,
> Sympathy and trust abounding.

No more falsehoods or derisions,
Golden living dreams of visions,
Mystic crystal revelation,
And the mind's true liberation.
Aquarius, Aquarius.

These words describe what would truly be the Kingdom of God— heaven come to earth. The word *Aquarius* literally means water carrier. To live in the Age of Aquarius means that we find the Water Carrier that connects us with the ocean of life, with ample peace, love, joy, and fulfillment for us and all our kind!

I assure you that my use of current astrological symbols as well as biblical symbols is no evidence that I have gone over to astrology! I must confess considerable skepticism and less knowledge about this most ancient of arts, or is it superstition, or science? Whichever it is, the fact that so many people of this time have adopted Aquarius to describe their hopes is a sign of the desperate search of secular man for meaning. Many have lost faith in the old words as a means of getting their bearings in a time when there is such rapid and threatening change. But hope springs eternal! And this is one of the best "signals of transcendence" pointing to the real hope. Indeed I believe this is the best day we have known in our lifetime to proclaim and live the Good News!

Actually, many youth and others today are in what Albert Camus calls "metaphysical rebellion." They are rebelling against a square world which limits life to the four walls of the physical senses— reality measured only by scientific gadgets, microscopes, and test tubes!

This rebellion at the evils around us and the megatechnology which simply magnifies them is being expressed in three ways, with the real possibility of a fourth, each evidenced by an eager willingness for some adequate discipline.

(1) Some are turning to *neomysticism*—gurus, Zen Buddhism, witchcraft, astrology, seances, even devil cults. This is a highly disciplined way, demanding hours of meditation and exercise, dietetic restrictions, etc.

(2) Others are mixing *psychedelic color, music, and drugs* in order to blast the senses. In gaining a few moments of ecstasy, they often threaten their very minds and lives. But here again, the most rugged disciplines are not too much. If death is likely in so many sudden and unjust ways and there is no meaning and purpose in life, why not live it up—do anything to get turned on, grasp as many moments of ecstasy or its nearest equivalent—no matter the cost. Here again the disciplines of the peer group require fantastic willingness to accept the most costly of disciplines, all in promise of another and higher "high"!

(3) Still others are the *new militants* who rightly refuse to believe that our world is the best possible world and are determined to "crush this ugly scheme of things entire and mold it nearer heart's desire." They are determined to smash the old and unjust, *now,* even if there is nothing ready to replace it. These groups, whether young or old, are the most disciplined of all. Their disciples are similar to those of the Communist cells and cadres of revolutionaries in other ages—united in their rage and determination to tear down to rebuild. To be a part of such movements requires the willingness to sacrifice time, money, even life itself to accomplish the ends accepted by all.

In all three of these approaches there are signals of wistful seeking, longing, hoping for the way, the truth, and the life. Sometimes the most violent nihilism is the most complete protest against the way life is, indicating some real conviction that it ought to be better. All have one thing in common: the willingness to discipline themselves in order to reach their objectives. The groups make their own rules, but all include strictest obedience to the groups' decisions or to the leader who knows the way!

The big question upon which life and the continuance of any kind of civilized existence depend is whether or not there will be adequate guides who know "the Way" and can share "the Life" and open up "the Truth."[13]

Will youth and adults possessing the Christian heritage misunderstand or reject it and cop out, or will we be able to help in the delivery of the new spirit in the new age? Will we join in the new song?

"The answer my friend is blowing in the wind"—the wind of the Spirit, creative, redeeming, blowing where it will—in vital new worship and meaningful community and worthwhile action, in living that is on tiptoe with expectation and creativity because of a conviction, a commitment, and a disciplined attention to fulfill the requirements for the new age!

This is the basic assumption of my faith: *there are streams of living water into which our human roots may go, through which we draw the grace and strength to live and act with nobility, dignity, courage, and wise, strong love. Therefore the putting down of these roots is the most important action of which the human mind and spirit is capable.* And the act of putting down these roots is what Christians have meant by the old words *prayer, worship, contemplation, recollection, meditation.* The old words describe the old pieties that have been abandoned by so many people who still cling wistfully to their old belief that God is like Christ.

This book will seek to dig beneath the old words and the old pieties to find the new song we all are longing to sing, and to help us to sing it with enthusiasm and joy, with great courage and hope. Only as we translate our faith into this kind of creative, life-bringing action made possible by meaningful disciplines will man ever stand up and begin to live in peace and love, "turned on to joy!" When this happens we really will have something to sing about!

Notes

1. Hugh T. Kerr, ed., *Readings in Christian Thought* (Nashville: Abingdon, 1966).

2. See Lance Webb, *When God Comes Alive* (Nashville: Abingdon, 1968), p. 28.

3. Thomas S. Kepler, *A Journey with the Saints* (Cleveland: World, 1951), p. 17.

4. These words are from the title of a book by Frank Laubach, the compassionate Christian missionary to the Philippines, who discovered over a quarter of a century ago the "Laubach Method," as it is called, of teaching illiterates to read. His program of "each one teach one" has spread through the world and enabled literally millions to read who without this approach would never have done so.

5. See Richard Collier, *The General Next to God* (New York: E. P. Dutton & Co., 1965).

6. Albert Schweitzer, *The Quest of the Historical Jesus* (New York: Macmillan), p. 403.

7. Ernest Gordon, *Through the Valley of the Kwai* (New York: Harper & Bros., 1962), pp. 77–78.

8. Ibid., pp. 112–13.

9. Ibid., p. 109.

10. I did not keep a diary of the external actions of each day. As explained in the preface, since 1947, I have been keeping a record of the things I read or experienced that spoke to me and my response to them.

11. The problem of appropriate symbols to represent the Reality we experience is a real one. It will be dealt with more explicitly in other parts of this book.

12. Bliss Carman, "On Love," *The Oxford Book of English Mystical Verse*, ed. D. H. Nicholson and A. H. Lee (New York: Oxford University Press, 1917), p. 458.

13. This writer is a member of the *Disciplined Order of Christ*— an ecumenical movement with the goal of developing personal and group disciplines in young and old that will cooperate with the Spirit in producing real Christian maturity. This movement is one of several such as Faith for Today and Yokefellows. Headquarters of the D.O.C. is P.O. Box 22103, Shaker Heights, Ohio 44122. The address of Yokefellows is Earlham College, Richmond, Indiana. Faith for Today is 279 Fifth Avenue, New York 10016. Such emphases are increasingly found in almost all churches today.

II
Disciplines
for the
New Age

3 The Song of New Perspectives

INSIGHTS INTO REALITY

It is not easy to sing a new song, or any song at all, in the strange land of megatechnology. How can we sing facing "future shock," loss of meanings and values in society, and personal losses and shocks that are always part of any life? Oh, there are various brave attempts—"Aquarius," "There's a New World Coming!", "On a Clear Day You Can See Forever," "This World Is Your World," and a flock of religious folk songs, secular and religious alike, filled with the universal themes of love, peace, joy, and hope.

We wish this were the Age of Aquarius with "harmony and understanding, sympathy and trust abounding." We long for the "clear day in which you can see forever and ever and ever." We hope and look for "the new world that is coming." But there is something missing. We *know* so much more than we *do*. There is a tragic gap between our scientific and technical knowledge and our human ability to perceive the crucial moral and spiritual insights needed for creative action.

THE NECESSITY FOR DISCIPLINES OF THE MIND AND SPIRIT

It seems to me that the priceless perspectives we crave can come only through a deeper insight into "grace and reality," and "grace and reality come through Jesus Christ" (John 1:17, Moffatt). It is true that many professing Christians would agree in principle, but unfortunately their lives remain unaffected. There is nothing attractive or helpful in their lives to convince and guide others. Why? Largely because most of us Christians are undisciplined.

59

Clearly all the tremendous developments of science have come about through intensive and dedicated disciplines on the part of individuals and groups. Think of Jonas Salk and his quest for the vaccine that would prevent polio—the hours and days, the months and years of preparation, of testing, retesting, failing, and trying again and again. So with the groups of researchers in NASA, seeking to develop the conditions in spacesuits and ships that would make travelers to the moon or to Mars safe and comfortable. Tens of thousands of hours and days spent by many thousand scientists, engineers, astronauts, all coordinated to the goal of landing on the moon—all of this patient and persistent discipline was required for a successful moon landing.

Just as the disciplines of science have given us insight into the requirements or laws of the physical universe, so the spiritual disciplines are the oft forgotten or denied requirements for the perspectives in our personal and social lives that will provide us with the needed insights into the "grace and truth" that came supremely in Jesus Christ and are reflected in the great procession of his followers in every age. The disciplines are the connecting links or roots by which such priceless perspectives come.

Look for a moment at the meaning of this word *discipline*. The dictionary defines it as "training that develops self-control, character, orderliness and efficiency . . . acceptance of or submission to authority and control." Submission to whose authority? Whose control? That is the primary question. Is it the authority that begins and ends in my own little god-self with all the dozen conflicting ego demands striving for mastery? Is it the authority of conformism to whatever little gods I accept from my peer group or the customs of my community that may temporarily give meaning and prop up my sagging self-confidence? Or is it the authority of the Lord of life with the way and the truth—the Spirit I meet in Christ through the human Jesus and in my own deepest insights—that I believe is in the very nature of things?

The authority that makes disciplines acceptable must be from *within* us, for to be effective, disciplines must be self-imposed. They must be voluntarily chosen rather than externally enforced. Self-imposed disciplines result in freedom, but a discipline imposed from the outside results in slavery. By our very nature we tend to rebel against such external impositions.

For instance, we are seeing a rebellion in our time against the rigid sex ethics imposed by puritanical customs. This rebellion in the form of sexual permissiveness has become so repulsive to many that the pendulum is swinging back toward what may be a more puritanical approach to sex. It is indeed against our very nature to accept enforced slavery to anything, whether it is the rigid demands of current mores in our society, the commands of a domineering father, or the demands of a stern and unbending God of wrath and judgment. "The fear of the Lord is the beginning of wisdom" (Ps. 111:10, RSV), says the ancient biblical proverb, but this fear is compounded of awe, respect, and a response to the self-giving love that in the Old Testament left the Israelites singing, "Thou art good and doest good; teach me thy statutes" (Ps. 119:68, RSV).

In this chapter we are to consider the deep roots, or connecting links, between our little human perspectives and the eternally true perspectives of Jesus Christ. These roots are grown or developed by the disciplines we accept voluntarily and wholeheartedly.

A good description of the undeniable need for such roots, or disciplines, may be found in a comparison of the people of Judah as they were preceding their fall and exile into Babylon and the people of our own scientific age with its threatening destruction. Read Jeremiah 17–18 for a description of the foolish way the inhabitants of Jerusalem and the little kingdom of Judah met the threats of the mighty power of Babylon. Their response sounds uncomfortably like that of secular man facing the dangerous problems created by the possession of the atomic bomb and other weapons our advance in science has placed in our hands.

After the Battle of Carchemish in 605 B.C., the Babylonians established their control over all Western Asia. Jeremiah's prophetic insight led him to warn his people and the weak and perfidious kings who ruled them during the next nineteen years that only a disciplined and obedient Judah would have the wisdom to act appropriately. It would take a strong and very wise people to live at peace with their powerful neighbor! Instead of discipline, however, they chose the way of escape—sexual and other sensual excesses. Deluding themselves in private attempts to be wealthy and secure, they were blind to the realities of their situation. Their delusions of grandeur, their foolish pride, and their religion expressed idolatry rather than a willingness to see and obey God's requirements for peace. Jeremiah did his best to warn them and bring true insight. "Turn back, every one of you, from his evil course; mend your ways and your doings. But they answer, 'Things are past hope. We will do as we like, and each of us will follow the promptings of his own wicked and stubborn heart'" (Jer. 18:12–13, NEB). They refused to listen to him. Judah did fall, and when Jerusalem was destroyed in 586 B.C., most of Jeremiah's people were taken in exile to Babylon.

The comparison with our times is striking. The dangerous threats of Babylonian power may be compared to the powers of the H-bomb and other destructive weapons, such as germ warfare, which are in the hands not only of America, Great Britain, France, and Russia, but now of Red China, Israel, and likely other nations. We too have forgotten the truth Jeremiah tried unsuccessfully to teach the people of Judah. Undisciplined excesses in food, sex, alcohol, and material things—to which we have added drugs, movies, and TV—and unbridled hatred and defiance of each other can but lead to a destruction so total it is unthinkable! Therefore we do not think about it. The *now* generation defines the mind of this age in a way strangely similar to Jeremiah's description of his people twenty-five hundred years ago in their time of futility and despair. Many of us could use his words to describe our attitudes. "Things are past hope. We will do as we like, and each of us will follow the promptings of his own heart."

Millions today would justify their attitudes and actions in words something like this: Things are really past hope. There is nothing we can do to change the evils about us, including scars on our subconscious minds left by our parents, grandparents, and the chains of the establishment—government, education, church, culture. Yes, things are past hope, for hope is itself a liar. Memory is unbearable because in both hope and memory there is a "no exit road" called "death." So I will live only in the here and now. I will live with innocence, spontaneity, novelty—all the pleasures I can summon. I will forget the past and ignore the future!

Obviously, we are responding to our feelings of insignificance, powerlessness, and meaninglessness in the personal and social realm just as the people of ancient Judah were. They too were surrounded by enemies. Then they were called Babylonians, Chaldeans, and Egyptians. Now they are called the war in Vietnam, the military requirements, or the Communists in China and Russia. Now as then there is no escape from our own finitude and frailty.

Jeremiah's answer to his people's futilities was sharp and to the point. "You follow the promptings of a wicked and stubborn heart." I'm sure they didn't appreciate this incisive diagnosis any more than we do. Do we really think our hearts are wicked and stubborn? No, it's the president, or the police, or the system, or the hierarchy, or the Communists, or the people over thirty, or under thirty, or the black militants, or the white racists, or the wife or the husband—not me!

What we need is a good view of this "heart" or "subconscious mind" which depth psychology can help us see, if we are not afraid to look. When we do look, we begin to recognize that indeed "the heart is deceitful and sick, who can fathom it?" (paraphrase of Jer. 17:9, NEB). The old versions use the word *wicked* here. Both words include rationalizations, false motivations, and unrecognized desires and values that are the hidden blocks in the channels of the water of life, cutting off the roots, so that we too have "rejected the fountain of living water" (Jer. 17:13, NEB).

The diagnosis is contemporary indeed. Consider this passage from psychiatrist Carl Jung's *Modern Man in Search of a Soul,* as he describes our human sickness.

> We have built a monumental world about us, and we have slaved for it with unequalled energy . . . and what we find when we look within must necessarily be as it is, shabby and insufficient.[1]

From his *Psychology and Alchemy* come these even more significant words describing our inner sickness:

> The great events of the world as planned and executed by man do not breathe the spirit of Christianity but rather of unadorned paganism. These things originate in a psychic condition that has remained archaic and has not been even remotely touched by Christianity. . . . Christian civilization has proved hollow to a terrifying degree; it is . . . veneer, but the inner man has remained untouched and therefore unchanged. His soul is out of key with his external beliefs; in his soul the Christian has not kept pace with external developments. . . . Christ only meets them from without, never from within the soul; that is why dark paganism still reigns there.[2]

Our first and greatest need is perspective insight—clear vision into ourselves as well as beyond ourselves to the Reality behind all realities which we call God. Therefore these roots, or channels, by which such perspectives come must be dug out, cut through, and opened up to let the true meaning, value, and power of life through. If our inner life is pagan, unchanged by our Christian or other good beliefs, it is not surprising that we do not live and act by them and that we are still in the heathen age of morality so wholly inadequate for the jet age of megatechnology!

Of course this is not the picture of human life as painted by those who glory in the freedom and grandeur of scientific man in this Age of Aquarius. Yet the tragic fact of human life with all our scientific know-how is that secular man has the power to make fruitful everything in the universe but himself. The sign of Aquarius is appropriately a symbol of the monumental world about us in which man has become the water carrier to bring life from the atom, oil from the earth, abundant harvest from the desert, food from the ocean, power from the sun—power for everything except to bring life to himself!

Yet even this power is awaiting us as a gift. But this gift is given only to those who trust themselves to something more than other men. It is for those who are open and willing to trust and be obedient in love to the eternal God. We recognize this truth immediately in the physical world as well as in the world of music and the arts. Handel, after hearing his *Messiah* played for the first time, cried exuberantly and gratefully, "It was not from me, it was from above." And Albert Einstein, when asked how he came by the theory of relativity, replied in utter humility, "It was given me. . . . He who does not pause to wonder or stand wrapt in awe is as good as dead. There is no life in him." The true scientist, according to Aldous Huxley, is one who is willing to sit down before the facts like a little child.

How strange that secular man has done this in every part of life except in the interior life from which all meaning, hope, joy, peace, and love come. Instead this inner life, as Jung puts it, remains full of "dark paganism" where the demons of hate, fear, greed, prejudice, and selfishness still reign.

What cannot man do? The woman at the well of Jacob in Samaria found the answer which modern man with all his sophisticated scientific knowledge is beginning to discover. According to the lucid story in the Gospel of John, one day when the disciples had gone into town to buy provisions, Jesus stopped by the ancient well which tradition says was dug by their ancestor Jacob two thousand years before. "A Samaritan woman came to draw water," says the record. Jesus startled her by asking, "Give me a drink." In the first place, she was a Samaritan and he was a Jew, and Samaritans and Jews were not on speaking terms, for the Samaritans were renegade Jews who had intermarried with the Gentiles and were despised by any intelligent, well-bred Jew. In the second place, she was a woman and strict rules forbade any rabbi to greet a woman in public. For a rabbi to speak to a woman, in public or alone, was a scandal and if known would end his good reputation. Besides, this woman was a shoddy character in the town—she had seven husbands! And yet Jesus spoke to her!

"What! You a Jew, ask a drink of me, a Samaritan woman?" she exclaimed in astonishment. Jesus replied, "If only you knew what God gives, and who it is that is asking you for a drink, you would have asked him and he would have given you *living water.*"

"Sir," the woman said, "you have no bucket and this well is deep. How can you give me 'living water'? Are you better than our ancestor Jacob who gave us this well?" That is, if the best Jacob could do was to dig a well and get water, how are you going to give me "running water," that is, fresh water from a stream?

Jesus answered her, "Everyone who drinks this water will be thirsty again, but whoever drinks the water that I shall give him will never suffer thirst any more. The water that I shall give him will be an inner spring always welling up for eternal life."

The woman then understood her own deepest question and its answer. *What cannot a man or a woman do? He cannot by himself draw water from the well of life, for he has no bucket with which to draw and the well is deep.* But water is there, as Jesus promised her. All who drink the water of physical, material accomplishment will thirst again, but whoever drinks the water Christ gives will never thirst. Instead there will be a spring of water welling up, bubbling over with eternal life. And by *eternal life* Jesus clearly did not mean only a life after death, but life that is eternal in quality and meaning *now.*

The man who is truly human has found the bucket to draw this

living water and uses it regularly, whether in the Age of Aquarius
or in the pre-Copernican age. He is the man who has learned to let
his roots go deep down within his own life and culture to the springs
of living water! We need to hear again the warnings of Jeremiah as
well as Jung. "A curse on the man who trusts in man and leans
for support [only] on human kind, while his heart is far from the
Lord! He shall be like a juniper in the desert; when good comes
he shall not see it" (Jer. 17:5–6, NEB). What a universal description
of the human experience. Trusting only in himself and other men,
man cannot see the good in self-giving, suffering love, in self-
sacrificial cooperation with his neighbors that alone brings true
peace and full, joyous life. Secular man in his search for the goods
of life misses the true good. For example, many parents who found
difficult times making a living during the depression determined
that their children would not have to struggle so much for their
material needs. They have lavished these "things" on their children
only to find that their children are often unappreciative and are
lacking in the true values of life which their parents had no time
to share!

To summarize this cogent parable of life, let me paraphrase
these words of Jeremiah.

> Deep rooted is the life who trusts in God—
> The living Reality in whom he lives, moves and has his being.
> The man of faith is not famished and starving
> in a salt land where no man can live.
> He carries water through deep roots from the streams
> of Grace which never run dry.

*What are the spiritual roots which man with all his science still
needs to let grow deep down into the springs of living water?* One
thing clear from the beautiful symbolism that is found so many
places in the Old and New Testaments is that this water is found not
in isolation but in a free fellowship with others.

The water is the grace of God—the word *grace* meaning the
undeserved, unearned gift of the gracious Father-Creator. The
Judeo-Christian faith declares that the spirit of insight, wisdom,
love, and compassion is the very presence of the Holy Spirit,
Immanuel, "God with us."

The springs of living water are the springs of *perspective* which give understanding and insight into the reality that is really valuable and eternally good. The *roots* by which these springs are reached are the roots of our conscious and unconscious human relationships with the eternal Giver of Life whom Jesus called Father.[3] Through him and his beloved son Jesus Christ, we are able to enter into a loving relationship with our fellow-man as we all share in his Spirit and drink of his living water that flows so freely.

The roots may be described by old familiar words: worship, prayer, communion, meditation, adoration, confession, petition, intercession, thanksgiving, commitment, obedience, service, giving, and acting in his name. But these words need to be reinterpreted today because for many people they are dead and meaningless. Nevertheless, they represent a primary necessity for every person, and if we stop using them and the methods they signify, we will have to get some new words and new methods that will have the same effect.

For, to summarize our human situation, there is no living water of loving, trusting relationships without roots that go deep into our relationship with our Creator-Father-Spirit and with those who through the centuries have known this relationship. There are no roots without conscious intent, that is, conscious willingness to discipline ourselves regularly in the use of our intelligence as we seek to learn from those who have gone before and to practice the acceptance of ourselves in the presence of this Christ Spirit in whom we live and have our very being. From such living relationships come the insights and perspectives without which we find ourselves "dwelling among rocks in the wilderness, in a salt land where no man can live!"

Our predicament here is in two parts. First, we dislike discipline, defined as steady, regular, consistent, continuous attention in practice by thought, words, and acts. The word itself has an offensive sound especially to a permissive generation. For we want to do as we like, when we like, following the promptings of what Jeremiah called "our deceitful, evil and stubborn hearts." "All we like sheep have gone astray," wrote the prophet Isaiah, "we have turned every one to his own way" (Isa. 53:6, RSV).

Remember the parable of the one sheep who, being smarter than the other sheep, despised the rest as "sheepish" in following the shepherd. Besides, he knew where the green grass was without the help of any shepherd. For a while he enjoyed his freedom. The grass was green and he was proud of himself. Soon, however, the grass gave way to a thicket with brambles in which the sheep was lost. The thorns pierced his wool and he was hungry and cold. He could no longer see either his fellow sheep or the shepherd. Suddenly, he looked around and saw the wolf coming. He turned in fear and started running as fast as he could, but the wolf was gaining on him, nipping at his heels. Then he found himself on the edge of a precipice. He had two choices: he could jump over the precipice or turn and face the wolf. This sheep did what many human sheep never do. He turned and faced the wolf. When he did, to his amazement he found it was not the wolf at all, but the shepherd's dog sent to bring him back to the green pastures!

This story is apocryphal, but it does represent our human dislike to be led and guided. It also depicts the tragedy that comes to so many who insist on always "doing their own thing." I have used this story with numerous counselees—alcoholics, marital sufferers, rebellious children and youth. Its value depends on how much confidence the one who goes his own way comes to have in the Good Shepherd. The discipline of following even him requires a conviction and a commitment as described in part one.

The second part of our predicament is that the words to describe the needed disciplines (or roots) of life are old words encrusted with wrong attitudes and approaches. Together they form what has been called *Christian piety,* and piety is not a very desirable word even to talk about, much less to accept and practice. (Who wants to be pious?) Piety has, like these other words such as *prayer, worship,* and *obedience,* been associated with so many false approaches to life and its meaning.

Of course, there are many different kinds of piety: Christian, Moslem, Hindu, secular, etc. There are also many kinds of Christian piety: Puritan, Victorian, Methodist, Amish, Roman Catholic, Lutheran, etc. Today social action piety is all the rage. If you are opposed to war and to racism, then adultery, drunkenness, and even dope addiction are acceptable or at least tolerated. This is the opposite, of course, of the piety of the average Christian who may not be too concerned with war or racism, but is horrified at sexual deviations or by what a person drinks or smokes. In addition there is the piety of a moralism based on certain absolute principles (from the Bible or from the culture about us).[4] As James Whitcomb Riley described it, "The meanest man I ever saw allus kep' inside o' the law!" There is the rather generalized Christian piety of religious duties—go to church, pay your part of its upkeep, say your prayers, and read a few verses from the Bible at the breakfast table or before going to bed at night. There is also a hedonistic form of piety which agrees with Ernest Hemingway, "Anything that's pleasurable is good; anything that's painful is bad."

Now, since it is so easy to misunderstand the authentic meaning of *piety,* why use the word at all? For the simple reason that it is a meaningful word if we use it to describe the pattern or style of being and doing that which we have chosen because of our own particular interpretation of faith; that is, our piety is the style of life, the things we do or don't do, which results from what we really believe is ultimate or, at least, most important.

Whether or not the disciplines recommended and described in this book for life in the Age of Aquarius will stand the test of our times is the one question that matters. We will not know whether they will or not until we have tried them. If the life patterns described here work for secular man in producing the harmony, joy, peace, and self-giving love that make him willing to cooperate for the well-being of all, there must be *water* there! This to the scientifically minded person is all the evidence needed. It is hoped these pages may open up the plugged channels that lead to the rivers of the water of life for many in the *now* generation! *The crucial test is whether or not we find water! If we want the fruits, we must want and develop the roots also.*

DISCIPLINES THAT LEAD TO NEW PERSPECTIVES

Christian prayer and worship, as practiced by Jesus throughout his life, point to the ways any of us may find the perspectives we need. Such prayer and worship along with their accompanying disciplines of meditation, silence, contemplation, reading, and sharing with others are the most costly action and priceless privilege known to man. They display the most creative, life-transforming perspective of which a human being is capable. Through them our spiritual roots may indeed reach the rivers of living waters and produce life with a new song in spite of the worst circumstances.

I said something like this in one of my addresses and was immediately dared by one of my hearers to prove my statement. Does the developing of spiritual roots of genuine faith in a regularly disciplined, intelligent approach to life *really* produce a life of love, peace, joy, and positive action in spite of the worst circumstances? I answered without hesitating, "Yes, I have found it so, and I can tell you of many others who know it is true."

"All right then," said my doubting friend, "how about a young person with cancer? I dare you to show how the spiritual disciplines of faith could do anything for such a person."

I responded with the story of a beautiful young woman of thirty-five, radiant, with an infectious gaiety and kindness that made her loved by many friends and adored by her husband. True she was somewhat spoiled by the adulation, but in general she remained a naturally free and loving person. Although members of the church I served, she and her husband were generally too occupied with parties on Saturday night to get up for worship on Sunday. But one day I was called to visit her in the hospital where she had undergone a hysterectomy.

When I entered the room, her face was the picture of despair. She had forced her doctor, who was also our mutual friend, to tell her the whole story. Yes, she had a malignancy. Yes, they would give her radium treatments, but the chances were ten to one against her recovery.

After she had told the story through many tears, she flared in anger, "Lance, I can't stand to think of what's ahead! Anything but cancer! What right does a good God have to permit such an affliction in me? I'm too young."

Bitter and humiliated, she resented God, life, and her husband. Then she calmed down and, with a piteous cry for help, said what any normal, secular-minded person would say in such a situation.

"Tell me how I can meet it, but don't ask me to pray about it. And don't tell me how its going to develop my character! I don't want to die. I want to live!"

I won't go through the long hours of conversation which we shared together over the next few weeks. I told her about the nature of God as I believed he is revealed in Jesus Christ and the framework of frailty with freedom in which we are to be reconciled to him.

Through her eagerness and openness she began to understand the meaning of prayer as Jesus prayed—prayer that is a response and a relationship and not a magical attempt to master the powers of the universe for our own benefit. She learned prayer as the way to new perspective and illumination resulting in honest combat with God and her self-demands.

One day she submitted, not to me or to a vengeful God, but to the loving purpose of a Heavenly Father whom she could not understand but whom she could trust. She did not have answers, but she had *the* answer—a confidence in the Eternal Love that held her in life and in death. When she said yes to the greatness and majesty of a love so great that even the cross could not defeat it, she won the victory over her own bitterness and resentment and then over her fears. She discovered that "perfect love banishes fear" (1 John 4:18, NEB).

I have never seen a more remarkable change take place in the mind and spirit of any person. She was as eager as a child packing for a long journey to a beautiful mountain resort. I could not tell her what was ahead because I had not been there and knew no one who had. I could not even give her definite proof that it was there. I did lead her through the thinking of great spirits such as St. Francis, John Wesley, the Apostle Paul, and the writer of the Book of Revelation.

Her little body wasted away until she was a bit of wrinkled skin and bones; yet from that body her spirit shown like an incandescent light. Her husband and her friends were the most astonished at the new Peggy. She talked with them freely and unaffectedly about her faith and the future. Her utter lack of fear and her patience under the indignities and pains of her illness made her seem like a bright ray of hope in a darkened world full of the heavy mists of hopelessness and despair. Hers was a perspective on life that opened the door for her friends who had valued pleasure and things above all else. Now they saw meanings and values that were to change their whole approach to life. A community of hopeful new believers resulted, and the circle of friends among whom she had moved lost much of its artificial gaiety and became a circle of love and joy.

At her memorial service there was a light shining through her
life and witness that no darkness could put out. I can honestly say
that I learned more from her than I have from almost any other
person I ever knew—in a short six months! But what of the length
of life when seen through the perspective of faith? It is eternal!

Perspective is the way you look at things. Do you see life as
the cat who went to London to see the queen but came back telling
only of the mouse under her chair? Or do you see it as a human
being who audaciously believes in some strange but real way that
he is a son of the mighty God, Creator and Father of all this multiverse with its billions of galaxies of suns and stars and, as many
astronomers declare possible, hundreds or even thousands of planets
where life is much further developed than on our earth?

True perspective is the capacity to see things in their *true relationships,* the ability *to discern* what is *primary* and what is *secondary.*
On the other hand perspective may be false, partial, twisted, and
illusory. It may be as inadequate as the perspective of a flea in the
wrinkle of an elephant's skin. Every time the elephant takes a mud
bath, no doubt the flea thinks the world is coming to an end!

How desperately we need a true perspective from which to see
ourselves and our world with our poor overburdened, anxious,
striving, self-pitying, frustrated, and depressed lives! We need to
see things as they are in the light of reality as God sees us, not as
our little ego-centered selves would see them! This requires the
ability to see above ourselves which is our holiest and most precious
possibility as human beings.

We need what the old Southern preacher had, who, in spite of the
loss of his family in a fire and a multitude of troubles, was the
most cheerful person in the community. When someone asked him
how it happened, he said, "Well, I'll tell you. When I begin to feel
sorry for myself, I just crawl upon a fence and watch myself pass
by and I just die a'laughin.''[5]

Christian prayer and worship at their best are that fence on
which even the most despairing of us may crawl and begin to see
things we never saw before. It is here that we find the power to
sing a new song, to laugh at our follies and fears, and to begin a
new approach to life.

This ability to put ourselves in conscious, intelligent relationship
to God resulting in an increasingly true perspective is genuine Chris-

tian prayer and worship as countless great spirits through the centuries testify. It is not some difficult game of manipulating God, of getting him to do what we want. It is not an escape, not wasted breath and time, but it is the power to see the truth about ourselves and our world, to accept it, and to act on it with joy and victory. As Dag Hammarskjöld expressed so clearly,

> How could this moral sense [upon which society depends] have escaped withering away, had it not constantly been watered by the feeder-stream of power that issues from those who have forgotten themselves in God?[6]

These are not the words of a misty-eyed religious fanatic but of one of the most creative, well-integrated, and fearless statesmen of the twentieth century.

The potent power of true perspective is the one thing so often missing in our lives and society and even in the life of the church. This is the reason for the crisis in so many of our homes and cities, in our nation and world, as well as in the church. For even in the church we have division, discouragement, crippling doubts, a strange cannibalism where Christians, members of a family, and citizens peck, peck, peck at each other with the absurd idea that the best way to save the nation or the church or the home is to destroy it. We have hostile gaps between citizens and government leaders, between clergymen and laymen, conservatives and liberals, advocates of social action and individual religion, between young and old, black and white, between those who emphasize worship and those who push action. All such cannibalistic self-destruction would be impossible if we really agonized over the true issues and needs and understood the motives of people we condemn and seek to destroy by words if not by guns. This lack of true perspective results in losing the very things we love most. Here is the tragedy of a father and mother separated from and cursing the hippie son or daughter whom they feel has betrayed them. Here is the pastor or lay member of the church rejecting and destroying the church without understanding that it can be redeemed and redemptive! How lacking in insight when we fail to see with Paul that "if you bite and devour one another take heed that you are not consumed by one another" (Gal. 5:15, RSV).

The strange paradox of the church, as well as of other institutions of our society, is that never have so many pastors and members, leaders and citizens worked harder for their ideal with less results! Something essential is missing. What is it? Some say, "Work harder, get with it." Certainly those who say they believe in the love of God and man need to realize more clearly that to accept this love means sacrifice and effort. But the real truth is that the word *sacrifice* is almost gone from our vocabulary. We do not seem to be willing to pay the price to bridge the gaps, to be reconcilers, to act with love, and even when we do work, it is devoid of power, meaning, and joy. Our work is often ineffective because it is done out of a sense of duty rather than out of overflowing love and confidence. We are lacking the song of new perspective of the grace and truth in Christ. As a result of our lack, the gaps are wider, our frustrations and futility more pronounced, and our doubts and cannibalistic infighting more destructive.

Our ambivalence is described in an interview between an editor of *Psychology Today* and Arthur Koestler, former Communist, now playwright, author, and philosopher. Arthur Koestler was asked about the two different approaches to changing man and society which he had been quoted as calling the approach of the *yogi* and the *commissar*. He answered:

> The Commissar is best described as the man who believes that change must be imposed by institutions, that we can cure everything from constipation to the Oedipus complex by reorganizing society. Along with this goes the belief that the end justifies the means and that we can reach our Utopian port if we rely on logical reasoning as a compass. The yogi on the other hand believes that all change must come from within the individual. He believes that the means alone count, that violence can never be accepted and that the magnetic pole of the Absolute will throw off the compass of logical reasoning. If we must boil it down to a single difference, call it Change from Within and Change from Without. All the rest comes from that.
>
> Neither method has ever been successful. One way leads to the Inquisition and the purges, the other to passive submission to the bayonet, to feces in the gutter and to trachoma.[7]

The editor then asked Koestler if it is possible to blend the two approaches, and he answered,

> We keep trying various forms of compromise, but we've never
> been able to synthesize the saint and the revolutionary. The yogi
> is concerned with the individual and the Absolute, the commissar
> with the individual and society. It's like asking a bird to become a
> fish.[8]

As I read his response, I wanted to ask Mr. Koestler if he had
never heard of Jesus or Paul or St. Francis or John Wesley or William Booth or Walter Rauschenbusch or Frank Laubach or Pope
John XXIII or Martin Luther King, Jr. Whatever you may believe
about any of these, the fact is that their action in the world to
change it toward justice and opportunity for others came from their
interior disciplines of prayer and worship that gave them a powerful
perspective from which action in the world was possible and effective!

The synthesis between saint and revolutionary has taken place
in many times and places in human history. For such persons we
are forever indebted and for many more such persons we are in
desperate need. The synthesis is the result of the perspective of
Christlike love which unites the inner and the outer. Prayer and
worship combined with social action result in wisdom and constructive power rather than the opposite.

The crisis of today in church and government and home is due
to the lack of this perspective. In the church it shows most clearly
in two contrasting styles or emphases. The first emphasis is on
activism. The only thing important is acting for social justice. The
other style of church life is to feel that if such action is too costly
or undesirable, forget it and do "church work" such as bazaars,
committee meetings, and suppers.

The sad fact is that for many on both sides there is a complete
or near complete cessation of prayer and worship. Some try feebly
to continue the old pieties, but with great confusion as to their
meaning and value. Prayer and worship are dubbed "unscientific,"
"other worldly," "irrelevant," "a waste of time and energy." Get
with it and do something.

This approach is like the story of the people in a lifeboat which
was pitching about in the high waves and near to going under. One
young man cried, "Let us pray." The tough old bosun called, "Let
the little feller pray, but you man the oars!" So a great many would
say that there is no need or value in prayer and worship—"just
man the oars and get with it!"

Look where this has led us. So many have lost this greatest privilege and power—the understanding of who we are, the reality of the ruling love of God in Christ accepted and celebrated in life and action, the required balancing of interior and exterior, rational and irrational in human life.

This precious confidence in the deep reality of the love that makes all this possible enabled St. Francis to pray and live out his prayer with such profound influence on the Europe of his time.

> Lord, make me an instrument of Thy peace.
> Where there is hate, may I bring love;
> Where offense, may I bring pardon;
> May I bring union in place of discord;
> Truth, replacing error;
> Faith, where once there was doubt;
> Hope, for despair;
> Light, where was darkness;
> Joy to replace sadness.
> Make me not to so crave to be loved as to love.
> Help me to learn that in giving I may receive;
> In forgetting self, I may find life eternal.

Why are so many of us who call ourselves Christians such poor peacemakers, such poor reconcilers—open scandals and not so funny jokes to the world who hear our fine words and noble professions? We can fool neither ourselves nor the world. We really haven't been with it! Why? Largely because of our failure to understand and meet the crisis in prayer and worship which is really a crisis in faith. Why pray when God is not real? Why worship a dim globular blur or an integrating principle? Having lost the reality of God, many of us have lost our own identity—our true perspective. We want the "fruit of the Spirit . . . love, joy, peace, patience, . . . self-control" (Gal. 5:22–23, RSV), but so often we do *not* want the roots from which grows the fruit of the Spirit, or at least we do not know how to grow these roots.

My experience, like that of so many others who have found Christian faith the source of all hopeful action, is that Christian prayer and worship are not primarily an enigma or a problem to be solved. Rather they are privileges to be accepted and lived.

Without such realistic prayer the person who goes out to act, even at great cost to himself and others, may indeed succeed only in killing the things he loves. Paul described accurately the futility of social action when it is self-righteous. "I may give away everything I have, and even give up my body to be burned—but if I have not love, it does me no good" (1 Cor. 13:3, TEV). Such action without the perspective of honest, open, obedient prayer which makes wise, strong love possible will do no one any good, except perhaps the ones who profit temporarily from the actions. But often even the disadvantaged and the poor for whom we seek justice find more harm than good in our self-sacrificing acts.

Without adequate perspective, though our objectives are good, our means will likely be less than adequate and even harmful to ourselves and to our cause.

True perspective includes both love and justice. In the life of Christ and in the realism of human life, the two can never be separated. The teachings of Christ contain both; they are neither soft and sentimental nor harsh and dominating. Love without justice is naïve, and justice without love is destructive. A prophetic ministry by itself is always harmful unless it is joined with a pastoral concern in which love enables us to accept with mercy those who are unjust even while we seek to remove the injustice. The television special celebrating the 100th anniversary of Abraham Lincoln's death described Lincoln as "hard as a granite rock and soft as a drifting fog." Lincoln cared deeply for those whom the Civil War hurt even as he was in the middle of trying to bring it to an end and as he wrote the Emancipation Proclamation. Clearly, if there had been enough loving justice, there would have been no Civil War. How precious and how desperately needed is the perspective of Christlike love!

There is, therefore, no more destructive creature on earth than the self-righteous reformer who is narrow, vindictive, and unable to keep from killing the very thing he loves. The only other creature who is equally destructive is the self-righteous pietist who escapes from social action into a dream world of familiar piety and turns the whole mess over to God! Both the commissar and the yogi type, who lose what they really seek to gain, are antihuman.

We have life only when we realize that Christian prayer and worship are our finest work and that our work, no matter how well intentioned, is empty and futile without worship at its best. The two belong together and cannot be separated if we are to be ready for the song of new perspectives that can lead to creative action. Arthur Koestler is right. The saint and the revolutionary must be synthesized; but his hope for combining the two by finding a pill[9] which we can swallow that will unite the inner and outer brain of a person, thus disciplining the brutish selfishness and passion that prevent loving cooperation, would be laughable if it were not so sad. Salvation by chemistry or electronics is a hopeless booby trap, a vain detour that fails because it depersonalizes both man and the Source of Life. Reality is not impersonal at the center, which might be given the name God, nor in the billions of small yet living units which we call "human beings"—"man."

PERSPECTIVES ON PERSONAL RELATIONSHIPS

Seeing the love, the quality of joy, the creative peace, the victory over temptation and evil in Jesus' life, his disciples said, "Lord, teach us to pray" (Luke 11:1, NEB). In other words, they were saying, "Teach us your secret. Tell us how to pray as you do so that we may live as you do." And Jesus answered in the words which begin what is known as the Lord's Prayer. "When you pray, say, 'Father, thy name be hallowed; thy kingdom come'" (Luke 11:2, NEB). What did Jesus mean by these time-honored words? Countless books, sermons, and critical analyses have been written about them, and I shall not try to compete with these worthy undertakings. I do want us to look, however, at these familiar words to see what they say to us concerning the needed perspective for the personal relationships which include the highest, deepest reality we call God and the little realities of our human selves.

Coming to the truest perspective of reality is the first requirement for life in the Age of Aquarius. God is the name we give to the nature of reality at its highest and deepest—the center of all being. But what is this?

Jesus called this center of reality *Father* or *Abba,* the Aramaic word for daddy or papa or Ab, as the Hebrew child spoke it. What a breathtaking leap of faith! At once we recognize this word *Abba* as a symbol representing a mighty mystery. Perhaps you do not like the word *Father* because your father was a bad one. Nevertheless the fact that you can think of what a good father ought to be points to the validity of *Father* as a good symbol of highest reality. The nature of God—Reality in and through all—is indeed a mystery and can never be contained or described in any one word or set of words, much less in pictures. If we could put it into words or pictures, what we describe would not be God, but rather an idol, as indeed many of the words and representations of God have become.

One thing we do see: in the life and victorious death of Jesus and the continuing life of our risen Lord, we, by faith, can see God's intention! This is the heart and core of our Christian faith and commitment. God's nature and character and something of his ongoing purpose are supremely revealed in the human Jesus, in his earthly life, in his resurrected life over the centuries, and through his followers. Here we believe is a true perspective on our own lives. As the Roman Catholic theologian Professor Edward Schillebeeckx puts it in the now classic book *Christ the Sacrament of the Encounter with God:*

> His human love is the human embodiment of the redeeming love of God. . . . The man Jesus, as the personal visible realization of the divine grace of redemption, is *the* sacrament, the primordial sacrament, because this man, the Son of God himself, is intended by the Father to be in his humanity the only way to the actuality of redemption. . . . Personally to be approached by the man Jesus was, for his contemporaries, an invitation to a personal encounter with the life-giving God, because personally that man was the Son of God. Human encounter with Jesus is therefore the sacrament of the encounter with God.[10]

When we pray *Our Father* we mean at least that the ultimate mystery behind all things is concerned about us, is better, wiser, and stronger than the best human father. Therefore the truest relationship between us and God is *trust,* the kind of trust that Jesus had in the worst moments, even on the cross, as well as in those beautiful days on the mountainside. Our highest privilege and gift is to possess this trust and to see ourselves and the true value of our fellow-men. Surely none of us who from his heart says "Father" can conceive of God as one who would do less for us or treat us worse than we would our own children! This is clearly what Jesus meant when he said, "If you then, who are evil, know how to give good gifts to your children, how much more will your Father who is in heaven give good things to those who ask him!" (Matt. 7:11, RSV). "Or what man of you, if his son asks him for bread, will give him a stone? Or if he asks for a fish, will give him a serpent?" (Matt. 7:9–10, RSV).

"Nothing can be good in him which evil is in me," cried Whittier. And so by faith we pray with our Lord, "Our Father, who is in the heaven of reality, hallowed, reverenced, adored be your name, your character, your purpose."

The supreme question to which the answer of our Christian faith gives priceless perspective is this: does the impersonal and non-rational rule and thereby frustrate the personal and the rational in our human existence? The basic insight which the prayer of our Lord declares is Good News indeed: We are members of the human family and truly akin to the Father Spirit who rules this universe, the gracious but strong Father of our Lord Jesus Christ. We are related personally in a personal universe. And we have a song to sing that lifts us out of self-pity and futility to hope and joy and love!

This is truly the crucial affirmation upon which any significant life depends. But how can we be sure? In the very same way we are sure of the love of our human father, mother, or any other human being. This is, *by being with them.*

"Oh," you say, "that is too simple. We can see them, but God is unseen and incomprehensible." True up to a point. The Old Testament does speak of God who is hidden. "Clouds and thick darkness are round about him" (Ps. 97:2, RSV). "How long, O Lord? Wilt thou hide thyself for ever?" (Ps. 89:46, RSV). "Oh, that I knew where I might find him, that I might come even to his seat! Behold, I go forward, but he is not there; and backward, but I cannot perceive him; on the left hand I seek him, but I cannot behold him; I turn to the right hand, but I cannot see him" (Job 23:3, 8–9, RSV).

Indeed when Alexander the Great conquered Jerusalem, the first thing he did was to enter the Temple to see this Yahweh, the God of the stubborn people he had vanquished; but to his amazement and disgust there was nothing to be seen. Their Yahweh was invisible! Rightly so, for the inspired people of the Old Testament refused to have any image or picture of God and much of the time they did not even use a word to describe him. When Moses encountered God at the burning bush and asked by what name he should be called in warning Pharaoh, he was told, "I AM; that is who I am. Tell them that I AM has sent you to them" [or "I will be what I will be"] (Exod. 3:14, NEB).

Then "in the fullness of time," "The Word [that creates, sustains and cares for all things] became a human being and lived among us. We saw his glory, full of grace and truth. . . . No one has ever seen God. The only One, who is the same as God and is at the Father's side, he has made him known" (John 1:14, 18, TEV).

As the early disciples of Jesus looked back over his life and the meaning of his death and resurrection, they were sure of one thing: he was a man among men. In his humanity there was something priceless being said and done. It was left to the aging John, writing in the Gospel bearing his name, to summarize most clearly the significance of Jesus whom they believed to be the Christ. John used the name the *Word* for the creating, sustaining, caring God of all things as he described what had happened in Jesus.

Yes, God is hidden in his fullness and glory for no mere finite man could bear to see God in his complete totality. Even the God of our Lord Jesus Christ is still infinite mystery, unfathomable in all his glory. He is "not to be encountered in the way in which we encounter other human beings."[11] But what these words about the encounter with the human Jesus as the visible representation of the invisible revealing the nature and purpose of God tell us is that the mystery of the hidden and unseen God is of the same kind as that of the mystery of human personality. For "are we so sure that we really do encounter the neighbor?"[12] For what we see when we see our loved ones in visible form is not the deepest truth about them, but only the external. We do not see the essence, but only the manifestation of the loved one's nature—his character, his attitude, and his acts. As Joseph Pieper in *The Silence of St. Thomas* says it, "The creature as creature is mystery to us, and somewhere, I think, St. Augustine has said that it is only in eternity that we will really see the neighbor, when we see him in God."[13] But we experience him as we are with him and witness his acts, hear his words, feel his touch. We come to know the real person through what he does and says. "It is in his body and through his body that a man is open to the outside and that he makes himself present to his fellow man."[14]

Through the centuries there have been human personalities that

were translucent with the light of some reality greater than themselves. The love of St. Francis made the love of Christ a reality for
countless thousands because he so completely identified himself
with the love of the human Jesus. Arthur Shearly Cripps pictures the
meditation of Francis, alone on the mountain, as he concentrated his
attention on the Christ on his cross. Having read over and over the
Gospel account of the human Jesus, now he saw him on a mighty
crucifix extending from one side of the heavens to the other. "What
art Thou, dearest Lord, and what am I, Vile worm and worthless
dust?" Later he tried to tell the answer he received as he waited
in loving adoration. To his little brothers he said that he would tell
them all he could, "and yet I leave you but the husk of it."

> I felt his Heart to beat within my heart
> It seemed He lent His Sacred Heart to me:
> One moment did I know His wish, His work,
> As if my own they were, and knew with them
> The worm-like weakness of my wasted life,
> My service worthless to win back His world. . . .
> I knew in blissful anguish what it means
> To be a part of Christ, and feel as mine
> The dark distresses of my brother limbs,
> To feel it bodily and simply true,
> To feel as mine the starving of His poor,
> To feel as mine the shadow of curse on all,
> Hard words, hard looks, and savage misery,
> And struggling deaths, unpitied and unwept. . . .
> The weary manner of their lives and deaths,
> That want in love, and lacking love lack all. . . .
> The woe of things we make our brothers bear,
> Our brothers and our sisters! In my heart
> Christ's Heart seemed beating, and the world's whole sin . . .
> O Heart of Jesus, Sacred, Passionate,
> Anguish it was, yet anguish that was bliss,
> To love them heart to heart, each selfish heart,
> To clasp them close, and pray in utter truth—
> 'Father, forgive, they know not what they do.'[15]

If you have ever had anyone near you who loved with even a
small part of such love, you would know as I do that the human
word spoken by that person is indeed the Word of the Eternal Love.

Whatever the meaning of the stigmata, the signs of the nail prints on the feet and hands of Francis, his life truly bore the marks of Jesus. In him Jesus lived all over again and through him lived the Eternal Love of God! So with every person who submits himself willingly and obediently to the spirit of the Christ.

I think of my mother who continued to identify her life with Christ from the earliest time I knew her until her death at the age of seventy-six. As I think of my own belief in the love of God, I am sure it was mediated to me first of all through her. When I was a baby, she held me in her arms and prayed that God's love would be seen in my life, whether as a minister of Christ's gospel or in whatever vocation I chose. But she never told me this until at the age of eighteen I wrote her of my decision to live by faith in Christ and to study for the Christian ministry.

She never failed to write or to share with me when I was with her something of her vision of the needs of the world and of what Christ could mean if only people understood. She made no parade of her faith, but many times I came upon her praying and saw a light on her face, sometimes tears in her eyes, and I knew hers was a real encounter with a Reality greater than she could describe or I could ever understand.

So the mystery of who God is and what love is may be known with assurance in our experience of him—his manifestation in his son Jesus Christ and in those who have caught his spirit. So *Christian prayer and worship are being with God, our Eternal Father, as revealed in Jesus Christ, in acts of intelligent faith.* There may or may not be the desired feeling though feelings generally follow. Ecstasy and visions are not the proof, for prayer and worship are acts of faith as we are with God in the encounter with Christ whose spirit is mediated to us through the human Jesus and through others who have lived in his spirit. We call this encounter prayer on the individual side and worship on the corporate side as we join with others in seeing with our spiritual sight and celebrating and acting on what we see.

THE TRUE PERSPECTIVE ON WHO WE ARE

The perspective on who God is, revealed in his Son, gives us the priceless perspective on who we are. When you pray, say, *"Our*

Father." What a world of difference when we say *our*. There is no life of freedom and joy in isolation, but only in loving mutuality. The sweet mystery of life is wise, strong, giving love. "For the whole law is fulfilled in one word, 'You shall love your neighbor as yourself' " (Gal. 5:14, RSV). "Love those who hate you, love even as I have loved you"—thus we may summarize Jesus' perspective on our fellow-man derived from his faith in the Father!

True mutuality of love is possible only as our own masks are torn off and as the walls of distrust, suspicion, and hostility are torn down between us. And this is possible only as I love and trust you as I know you love and trust God. The fact is that we cannot love others and ourselves rightly unless we are loved by one who is greater and higher than we. To be able to see into other persons' needs and hurts, to be merciful, kind, and constructive when we dislike and even hate their evil actions, and then to love them is the first necessity for life and peace in the home, in the church, between races, and in the world. It comes only as we accept ourselves as loved and forgiven by God. In the security of this love then we may love. The word *love* as used here does not mean sentimental affection but mutual respect, strong, wise, constructive, self-giving good will even when the persons loved are unlovable, even hateful! Possessive, desiring love alone destroys; wise, strong, giving love creates.[16]

Alan Paton in his book *Instrument of Thy Peace* uses the prayer of St. Francis to make one of the clearest statements I have read on the necessity for the right kind of prayer as the channel to becoming an instrument of peace in the world. In his prologue he says he is writing

> for those who do not wish to be cold in love and who know that being cold in love is perhaps the worst sin of them all; for those who wish to keep their faith bright and burning in the dark and faithless world.[17]

He admits that he is in

> unrepayable debt to Francis of Assisi, for when I pray his prayer, or even remember it, my melancholy is dispelled, my self-pity comes to an end, my faith is restored, because of this majestic conception of what the work of a disciple should be. So majestic

is this conception that one dare no longer be sorry for oneself. This world ceases to be one's enemy and becomes the place where one lives and works and serves.[18]

Why this creative response? Because we accept ourselves as loved by the steadfast love, and therefore we are not primarily concerned about getting other people to love us. Surely that is the heart and secret of true perspective so desperately needed in our human lives today.

The trouble is we all have a *ladder* of *sins,* or whatever name you want to call our deceitful, selfish, proud, and hurtful attitudes and acts. Oh, we may not be on the top rung of this ladder with the great saints, but neither are we on the bottom rung! We look down on those beneath us for after all there is always somebody much worse, we think, and to gossip about them somehow makes us feel better. Self-righteous morality (looking down on others) is as harmful, and sometimes more so, as the lower, more obvious sins.

One of the most significant statements I have heard recently on this subject was made by an eloquent black preacher. His perspective was truly one of Christlike love as he described a tragedy. Many white Christians who have quit hating Negroes have substituted hatred for white people who hate Negroes! Self-righteous morality without love has canceled the possibilities for good in much of today's civil rights laws just as it did for yesterday's prohibition laws. There is no other way to solve the racial problems in our world— or any other problems of human relations—except through the perspectives of humble Christlike love. And when this black preacher pleaded with both white and black as members of the family of God to "break bread" for all the needy, he was prophetically articulating this truth.

Jesus said to the most religious people of his day, the Pharisees whose morals were impeccable according to their interpretation of the law, "Truly, I say to you, the tax collectors and the harlots go into the kingdom of God before you" (Matt. 21:31, RSV). No wonder they were angry, for they, like us, did not like to have their ladders of superiority torn down.

We need a perspective to see ourselves as we are in God's sight. But the trouble is our perspectives are always so partial; we have only a knothole view of life! So often like Snoopy who lies on top of his doghouse viewing the whole world in superior disdain, we do not recognize the difficult truth about our own lives. From a true perspective, we are able to be honest before God, ourselves, and others.

PERSPECTIVES THAT BRING LIFE OR DEATH

Only when I see myself in the mirror of Christ's loving goodness do I see the infinite possibilities of my life, only about one-twentieth of which will be realized at best unless I have an adequate discipline of prayer and meditation and worship with full openness to truth. Then and then only am I able to pray with honesty and wholehearted commitment, "Thy kingdom come, thy will be done in my life as in the realms of reality."

The fact we need now to recognize is that his kingdom has come, his rule is here, though it is not acknowledged and understood by most people. We come to see that the only way things will work is according to his will and way. This is the meaning of the old familiar words, "Our Father who art in heaven." Heaven is not only on some far-off star in the billionth galaxy. Heaven is wherever God is accepted and his rule obeyed. Hell is wherever God's presence is unrecognized. When I am unwilling to say yes to his purposes, and seek to rule myself, I am in hell—the insanity of self-centeredness. It is easy to see this in others, but difficult in ourselves. Only as we learn to pray and worship honestly in his presence and only as we are willing to burn up our favorite ladder of sins from which we look down on others can we be whole and free, able to help rather than destroy the things and persons we love most!

To pray "Thy kingdom come" requires surrender of *my* kingdom. The fact that I have not done this is my problem. This is the reason for the hurt feelings, the injured pride, and the pain so many "good Christians" have. Here is the reason the best-intentioned crusader, reformer, and revolutionary so often fails. "*My* Kingdom come. *My* will be done" is the prayer we really are praying, irrespective of the words we use.

Arthur Rhine gives an imagined conversation between the Lord and Cain which points to our tragic situation.

> The Lord says, "An offering from you, Cain?
> What do you bring?"

Cain says, "Of the fruit of the field."
The Lord says, "I gave you that, have you
nothing that is truly yours?"
And Cain says, "My arms and my limbs."
"All that was given you and will be taken from
you," said the Lord.
"What then is truly mine?"
"What you can keep forever."
"That would be nothing but myself," said Cain.
"Give me yourself," said the Lord.
"Alas, I love myself."

But this answer is only a dodge to hide the real truth. Cain did not, and neither do we, without a new perspective, love our true selves. It is this imagined picture of self that we love. We cannot truly love ourselves until we see that we are loved by God. Only when we love ourselves as he loves us can we quit fighting our true selves and pray that his kingdom will come in truth, in love, in peace—in me as in the heaven of reality!

One morning a thrush flew through the open door of my Vermont study and was frightened by my presence. Seeing the large picture window, she flew against the glass trying to escape. Time and time again she hurled herself against the glass only to fall back bruised and broken. I was unable to help her until finally she was so weak and hurt she let me guide her to freedom. As I watched her fly away I wondered, "Will not God do as much for me?" I recalled Jesus' words, "Fear not, . . . you are of more value than many sparrows" (Matt. 10:31, RSV). "And not one of them will fall to the ground without your Father's will" (Matt. 10:29, RSV).

I realized that this is a parable of every one of us, and of mankind. We are beating our life wings against the false glass of our own built-in picture of life which beckons with alluring promises of freedom from boredom, littleness, and rejection. The result of our struggles is only to fall back time and again, bruised and broken by the lovelessness, inferiority, hostility, and fear that come from our inability to see the truth about our lives and world. We are looking at life through the wrong perspective. No wonder people are rebelling at the rigidities of the perspective of materialistic science and megatechnology. Someday we will learn, perhaps through much suffering, that there is no way out through our own self-made windows.

It will be a happy day indeed when we stop fighting God and our true selves! We will become humble and secure when we are willing to be truly human. The Lord of truth and love will pick us up and turn us loose into the blue sky of freedom to be our true selves. We will lose our self-pity and hostility and begin to share with God in making our homes, our churches, our communities, and our world a place where his eternal, loving reality is acknowledged and accepted.

Such is the priceless meaning and privilege of prayer and worship as perspective. From them come illumination, acceptance, caring involvement, and sacrifice with celebration!

Our Father who art in heaven—the heaven of highest reality.
Thy Kingdom come—not mine.
Thy will be done—not mine, in my home and in my world.
As it is in all your great and glorious universe.

NOTES

1. Quoted by Douglas V. Steere in *The Hardest Journey* (Lebanon, Penn.: Sowers Printing Co., Pendle Hill Pamphlet No. 163, 1969, pp. 9–10.
2. Carl Jung, *Psychology and Alchemy.*
3. See pp. 78-81, 91-92 for an interpretation of this most familiar and often misunderstood symbol.
4. Cf. Requiem for a Lost Piety.
5. See Lance Webb, *On the Edge of the Absurd* (Nashville: Abingdon, 1965), pp. 74–75.
6. Hammarskjöld, *Markings,* p. 105.
7. Arthur Koestler, in an interview in *Psychology Today,* June 1970, p. 63.
8. Ibid.
9. In Koestler's words, a "neuro-psychopharmacological discovery."
10. Edward Schillebeeckx, *Christ the Sacrament of the Encounter with God* (New York: Sheed and Ward, 1963), pp. 14–15.
11. Christopher F. Mooney, S.J., ed., *Prayer: The Problem of Dialogue with God* (Paramus, N.J.: Paulist Press, 1969), p. 13.
12. Ibid.
13. Ibid.
14. Ibid.
15. *The Oxford Book of English Mystical Verse,* pp. 512–16.

16. For the difference in "desiring-love" and "giving-love," see Lance Webb, *Discovering Love* (Nashville: Abingdon Press, 1959).

17. Alan Paton, *Instrument of Thy Peace* (New York: Seabury Press, 1968), p. 7.

18. Ibid., pp. 11–12.

4 The
New Song
of Illumination

HONESTY BEFORE GOD THE REALITY

O happy day! It is a happy day when we stop fighting the God of reality, the reality of our true selves, and the reality of the universe as it is and not as we wish it were! For then, though it may have to be done in darkness and without visible sight or proof, we begin to say yes and amen to life. We demonstrate *"a willingness to let things be as they are* [at least as the given, the starting point]."[1] Then we are praying with Jesus: "The Son of God, Christ Jesus, proclaimed among you . . . was never a blend of Yes and No. With him it was, and is, Yes. He is the Yes pronounced upon God's promises, every one of them. That is why, when we give glory to God, it is through Christ Jesus that we say 'Amen' " (2 Cor. 1:19–20, NEB).

Saying yes through Jesus Christ enables us to accept ourselves as of "more value than many sparrows" (Matt. 10:31, RSV), as accepted and loved by God—amazing thought! Then we can stop trying to fly like a deluded bird through the window glass of our own self-centered values and demands. We are open to the truth, humble and secure; and, therefore, we are free to be our true selves. This miraculous transformation from slavery to freedom has happened to thousands in every age. It is taking place now in hundreds of youth who have been on heroin and other drugs. It is happening to countless adults who have been addicted to alcohol, race prejudice, and material things and who have grown old and weary fighting themselves.

How does this infinitely desirable state come to be in which

90

obviously life at its best is possible? To summarize what has been said before and to indicate another step: Christian prayer and worship at their best are the most creative and productive actions known to man. They are the roots of the tree of life that reach down to the rivers of living water. This living water is the grace of God who gives us our most precious gifts, especially the gift of a true perspective, the ability to see our lives and our world and others about us as they really are, as God sees them and not as we might picture them. This kind of prayer and worship makes us open to receive the gift.

In the last chapter we considered the insights given in the first part of the Lord's Prayer. For some professing Christians the words are worn slick with familiarity. They are thought of by secularists as old and dusty words from another world so unlike ours as to be of no value. *Abba-Father,* however, will never be an old dusty word so long as there are loving parents willing to sacrifice themselves in strong, wise love for their children. Indeed, I must reaffirm my choice of the highest symbols we can think of to represent the highest and deepest reality. Unquestionably, for me, the personal is infinitely above the impersonal, for the personal, the experience each of us is given, is the call to master and control the impersonal. So the word *Father* is a much more acceptable symbol than unconscious force or integrating principle. The biblical writers make this clear. "The government will be upon his shoulder, and his name will be called 'Wonderful Counselor, Mighty God, Everlasting Father, Prince of Peace' " (Isa. 9:6, RSV). " 'And his name shall be called Emmanuel' (which means God with us)" (Matt. 1:23, RSV).

These names in our scientific age of technology assume infinitely more value than in the relatively simple ages preceding. For the impersonal is crowding out the personal, and this is one of the main reasons for so much meaninglessness in secular man's life. Can you imagine anyone in the depths of frustration and despair crying out for help to such impersonal forces: "Oh, Integrating Principles, give me wisdom!" "Oh, Cosmic Powers, give me your strength!" It is the crass uncaringness of an impersonal universe that presents us with our central predicament! If the cosmic powers are to support and strengthen us, they must be considered at least as personal as we are, that is, able to think and to care! Of course, these are symbols. *Anthropomorphic* is the word for thinking like a man. But

how else can we think except in the highest symbols that have meaning to our human minds?

Therefore, these words—*Father, Counselor, Immanuel* (God with
us)—and the deep reality they represent are truly the best hope
for the people who sit in a greater darkness and the shadow of a
more horrible death than could have been imagined in the time of
Isaiah.

Megatechnics and its fallout of addiction to things, money, sex,
alcohol, or drugs leave us more vulnerable to despair than mankind
has ever been before. We have an aloneness in the vastness of our
multiverse that cannot be met by scientific or mathematical theorems
or engineering devices.

Hear then with reverence and awe the summation of man's
highest way of addressing and committing himself to God the
Reality.

> Abba-Father who is in the heaven of reality, hallowed, revered be
> your name of love, your signature of compassion as written in the
> very constitution of the universe, and supremely in the life and
> death of your Son on the cross of infinite love, but also written
> large in all human life—Your will, not mine, be done. Your king-
> dom, not mine, come!

Such an intelligent perspective on the highest Reality opens up
another of the springs of life which I am calling *illumination*—
light in our darkness. Costly light it is indeed, not only to God who
gives it, but to us who receive it, but most priceless and necessary
for constructive and loving life in any age!

How difficult it is to be honest with ourselves, not only when
we are young but even more so as we get older. How very little
we know of ourselves! How small indeed was Simon Peter's knowledge of himself! In the last hours with his teacher and friend before
Jesus' betrayal and crucifixion, Peter had bragged, "Lord, why cannot I follow you now? I will lay down my life for you" (John 13:
37, RSV). The record does not describe the scene, but I am sure
Jesus looked deep into Peter's eyes for a few moments as he answered
with compassionate but realistic understanding, "Will you lay down
your life for me? Truly, truly, I say to you, the cock will not crow,
till you have denied me three times" (John 13:38, RSV).

Can you imagine what went on in Simon Peter's mind both then and later as "the Lord turned and looked at Peter"? Peter was standing in the outer court of Caiaphas's palace, having denied his Lord just as Jesus had said he would! What agony of mind Peter must have had as his friend and master was dying on the cross and then was laid in the tomb! Tradition has it that his hair turned gray during these terrible hours. He realized not only the sufferings of Jesus, but for the first time he looked into the depths of himself and saw what he truly was—a miserable traitor to all that he really wanted to be and thought he was. He had not only denied his Lord, but he had denied what he knew was his true self!

The story does not end here, for him or for us. If it did, we would be creatures of unmitigated despair for we have all denied and betrayed our Lord and our true selves, over and over again. The story goes on to the scene by the lake that morning when Peter met the risen Lord. Jesus probably put his hands on Peter's shoulders and looked into his eyes as he said, "Simon, son of John, do you love me more than these?" (John 21:15, RSV). I think he meant, "more than these inner demands that you be a 'big shot,' successful, recognized, and important—do you really love me more than these? If you do, then feed my sheep."

From that hour Peter ceased his bragging, self-centered ways and became more and more the "Rock" that his new name implied. He was selected by the other disciples as their leader. Though the old "Simon" in his nature made appearances several times through the years,[2] Peter was faithful in feeding the sheep entrusted him by the Good Shepherd. Tradition tells of his martyrdom during the persecution of the Christians under Nero. As the soldiers proceeded to crucify him, the story goes, he asked that he be crucified with his head downward, "for I am unworthy to die as my Lord died."

Only when Simon, son of John, had become honest before God could he really become Peter the Rock, the son of God as Jesus saw him early in his discipleship! Only then could he truly pray with his Lord, "Our Father, thy kingdom come, thy will be done in me and through me, no matter the cost!" Only then could he become the mighty leader of the fearless, scattered band of disciples that began a new era of creative hope in the life of mankind!

Christian prayer and worship—meditation and thinking—at their best are accepting a truer perspective on our lives in the presence of eternal Love ruling all. Therefore such times are moments of illumination, when at last we get honest before God and see ourselves and our world more nearly in the light of reality.

Obviously most of us are like Simon Peter. Before we are ready for the costly prayer that brings illumination, we must go through suffering; but the suffering must be seen in the light of the love that did not stop even at the cross. For then and only then can we be willing to accept the pruning knife of the Divine Gardener. Jesus indicated this need in the parable of the vine and the branches which he taught his disciples in their last night together. "I *am* the real vine, and my Father is the gardener. Every barren branch of mine he cuts away; and every fruiting branch he cleans, to make it more fruitful still. . . . The withered branches are heaped together, thrown on the fire, and burnt" (John 15:1–2, 6, NEB). As Phillips translates part of this unusual parable, "Now, you have already been pruned by my words. You must go on growing in me [subjecting your lives to more pruning] and I will grow in you" (John 15:3–4).

Pruning time is a costly time. Anyone who has ever grown roses or grapes knows that when the leaves are permitted to luxuriate and continue growing without pruning, there will be few or no roses or grapes. The excess foliage must be pruned away. Humanly speaking, we do not like pruning. It hurts. This is the main reason there is so little truly honest prayer before the Christ Presence: we are afraid we will be hurt.

"Lord, a little pruning may be necessary, but surely not these beautiful branches! I am so proud of them. Surely not this! or this! or this!"

But God is the Divine Gardener who is neither dead nor on a vacation. He loves us so much that he will not settle for anything less than our fullest development. We are to bear the most abundant crop of love, joy, and creative peace, with patience and fortitude and concern, of which we are capable! For he knows that nothing else can really satisfy his own creative purpose for us, or satisfy us and the fellow members of his family.

The difference between us as persons and the rose bushes and the grapevines is that roses and vines do not have any choice as to whether or not they are to be pruned. As children of the Father, we have two choices: either to go voluntarily to the Divine Gardener's pruning so that we may be more fruitful, or to delay the pruning, put it off, seek to escape for awhile. But if we choose this last way, the forced pruning will come eventually as the loving judgment of the Divine Gardener who will not let us go fruitless. Surely the God Reality cares as much for us as a gardener does his vines!

This is indeed an appropriate parable of what is happening today in the Age of Pisces. During the past fifty years we have seen in our world the forced pruning of two world wars, the Korean War, the Cuban revolution, and the war in Vietnam. We have seen it in our broken homes, in crushed and wrecked lives, in many idealistic youth destroying themselves either in escape through drugs or nihilism. We see it in the church that often forgets its reason for being and even in our own lives that are often so miserable and destructive rather than joyous and creative. This is the forced pruning—the loving judgment of a righteous Father-Gardener!

Christian prayer and worship and the other disciplines of the devoted spirit, rather than being an escape, are ways of voluntarily asking for the Gardener's shears to prune away the unnecessary foliage and dead vines in order that we may produce more fruit of love and peace and joy! With these kinds of disciplines accepted gladly, the forced pruning is unnecessary. Wise indeed is the person who can say with the poet H. M. Corning,

> In February, when the sap's below the inattentive earth,
> I take my shears and prune away the too audacious years.
> It's grapes I want, not mere leafy show.
> So I trim the trailing year's growth to a span.
> It takes some fortitude to cut a vine,
> Cutting the heart a little as I cut mine;
> But since it's grapes I want, I understand how
> To rebuke the heart in order to fill the hand.

How does one "rebuke the heart in order to fill the hand"? The trouble is we do not know our hearts. We recall again Jeremiah's words, "The heart is the most deceitful of all things, desperately sick; who can fathom it?" (Jer. 17:9, NEB). None of us likes to believe that. Indeed, we have plenty of cheerful humanists to tell us that man is innately good. All he needs is better teaching, more information about himself and his fellow-man. But depth psychology, as I have previously pointed out, shows us the extent of our rationalizations and self-justifications, how we hide even from ourselves the real reasons for our negative, hurtful attitudes and acts. How easy to make ourselves believe that anything we want is good because we want it. As Jesus put it, "Wisdom is justified by all her children" (Luke 7:35, RSV).

How do we really get honest with ourselves before God who is the truth, the reality of life and of all things in this mysterious universe, who makes possible the glorious but costly illumination we need?

We gain the honesty by doing what Simon Peter did—putting Jesus Christ as Lord in the center of our attention. This is the reason Christians have always prayed, "through Jesus Christ, our Lord," "in the name of Jesus." For this is what Christian prayer and worship really are—getting a good look at ourselves and our world in the light of a "clear day." In honest prayer we subject our innermost thoughts, desires, attitudes, and acts, as well as the attitudes and acts of others, to the light of Christ—the light that shines inexorably into the darkest and murkiest corners.

What a tremendous difference in Simon Peter before and after the crucifixion! Before, the center of his attention was himself— his needs, his "must-haves," the demands of the little lord Simon whose deepest desires, conscious and unconscious, were to prove himself a big success in his own eyes and in the eyes of others, even to the little maid in the court of Caiaphas's palace! After the crucifixion and the terrible experience of seeing Jesus during his trial "turn and look at him," the center of Peter's attention was on Christ. In the light of Christ's look, Peter saw his little, unworthy, petty self as it really was. He hated what he saw enough to surrender it. Captured by the love of Christ he was able to become a new person—the "Rock" that Jesus had seen him as being.

Christian prayer and devotion—worship, contemplation, meditation—are meeting God in conscious, glad attentiveness in Christ.

First, we meet him in the story of the man Jesus who lived, loved, suffered, was crucified, died, was buried, and rose again, becoming through the will of the Father-Reality the "universal power as the Master of history, the Lord of the universe."[3] It is this concentrated attention by Christians of every age on the saving event centering around the human Jesus that has produced such results in the use of the *Spiritual Exercises* of St. Ignatius of Loyola and the other creative disciplines of prayerful reading.

> The gospels do not simply give cold facts about our Lord; they record his words and actions as understood, selected, interpreted and *lived* by these privileged witnesses to the faith of the apostolic Church. . . . Because the sacred text conveys this revelation about Jesus of Nazareth incarnated in the reaction of faith of its sacred author (and of the Christian community that stands behind him), it is capable of producing a similar reaction of faith in the twentieth-century believer. . . . The final step . . . is the religious experience, the "saving event." . . . *the mystery must happen for me, to me.*[4]

The world-wide popularity of the rock opera, *Jesus Christ Superstar,* has revealed the same amazing impact that has been repeated every time and place where the human Jesus has been encountered in any depth of realism. From the many stories of the remarkable influence of this best-selling album and its words describing Jesus' trial, crucifixion, and death, let me relate one that took place in a storefront community in Evanston, Illinois. The events were related to me by a young student from nearby Garrett School of Theology who had gathered there a group of youth, mostly addicts to drugs of various kinds. They were outcasts from their homes and society, but they were beginning to find a community of caring friends in which there was hope for meaning and love.

This young student leader described to me how they listened intently to the recording of *Jesus Christ Superstar.* They wanted it played over and over again, not primarily for the music though they enjoyed the strong beat. They wanted the answers to the questions of Mary Magdalene, Judas, and the crowd—questions which were now their own. They could see themselves in Simon Peter, Judas, Mary Magdalene, Caiaphas, Pontius Pilate, Herod, and the crowd. Their characters all stood out in sharp contrast with the spirit and life of this man Jesus.

"Was he really like that?" they asked him. "Read the records and see," he wisely answered. Having identified himself with them in loving concern, he was joined by them in spending many hours reading and sharing together the meaning of the gospel story. When they came to the part in which Jesus was described as praying and teaching the disciples to pray, they timidly asked, "Could we learn how to pray? Could we have a worship time together?" Their leader was wise to let them do the pushing though he sought to interpret as best as he could the early church's experiences and what they thought of Jesus. He sought to take them beyond the final words of Jesus dying on the cross to his early followers' experience of Christ who had been dead but was now alive and present.

As in all other ages many of these youth began to identify with the disciples who denied and betrayed Jesus. Hungry for true love like Mary Magdalene and Peter and the others, they are saying in his presence, "I've seen myself. I seem like someone else." They are becoming new creations in Christ. With the writer of 1 John they are beginning to say, "We love because he loved us first" (1 John 4:19, NEB).

The illumination of his love has brought the meaning and value of human life to light, and in that light each one sees himself not only as he is, but as he can be. All over the world today men and women are finding themselves—their true selves—in their personal and group encounter with Jesus Christ. They no longer need to depend on dope or alcohol or recognition or material success for life! "The mystery has happened for me and to me!"

This mystery—the new illumination resulting in the new creation —happens to us not only by concentrating our attention on the simple, loving human Jesus; but from the time of Pentecost, we, like the early Christians, find the events in the life, death, and victory of Jesus our friend revealing the infinite love and victory of the eternal spirit whom Jesus taught us to call "Father." The New Testament Christians used interchangeably the words *Christ,* the *Spirit of Jesus Christ,* and the *Holy Spirit* to indicate that the great Creator-Father had made himself known in the life and spirit of their friend Jesus, and that now in his risen life, this eternal Christ was near to them in the Holy Spirit. Their Christ and ours is the Lord of history who "directed the destinies of his church as well as of the entire universe."[5] The central conviction that moved the apostolic church, as it has vital Christians ever since, was "that Jesus Christ through his exaltation . . . has *not* been removed to some mythical existence beyond the furthest galaxy, but is *actually more dynamically present* in the world than ever he was when he walked the hills of Galilee."[6] He is not withdrawn but more actively and really present in the life and history of mankind than ever!

Christian prayer, therefore, is meeting the mighty God-Reality as made known in the historical man Jesus, who as the risen Christ is really present with us. He lives continually in our own spirits when we are open to him and in the spirits of the great and loving persons of all times and places.

There are two ways in which we open our spirits to him. First, by thinking, consciously meditating on his gracious goodness, his majestic greatness, wisdom, and love, the continuing Good News lives in those who have the same Spirit. The first part of all genuine Christian prayer and worship is conscious attention on the nature of God. The opening address of the Lord's Prayer indicates this. "Our Father who art in heaven, hallowed be thy name."

> There's a wideness in God's mercy,
> Like the wideness of the sea:
> There's a kindness in his justice,
> Which is more than liberty.
>
> . . . .
>
> For the love of God is broader
> Than the measure of man's mind;
> And the heart of the Eternal
> Is most wonderfully kind.[7]

Second, we meet him consciously by faith. "Speak to Him for He nears, and shall meet—Closer is He than breathing, and nearer than hands and feet."[8] Yes, but meeting him is no accident; we must consciously *will* to meet him. When our attention is joined with his, we have the precious illumination we need. We begin to see ourselves and to enter into the new creation, as the beautiful song in the popular musical, "On a Clear Day You Can See Forever," declares.

> On a clear day—
> Rise and look around you—
> And you'll see who you are.
> On a clear day—

How it will astound you—
That the glow of your being
    outshines ev'ry star.
You feel part of—
    ev'ry mountain, sea and shore.
You can hear, from far and near,
    a world you've never heard before.

. . . .

On that clear day—
You can see forever and ever and ever
    and evermore![9]

The truth of the illumined spirit is present in the words of this
song. But we are never told how to acquire it. This is the hub of
our problem. As the muscial suggests, some illumination may come
from hypnotism and psychiatry. But even the musical hints that
there is some deeper mystery, some more adequate source. Is it by
taking a trip on LSD or other drugs? Is it by the way of contemplation made popular by Zen Buddhism? This is not the place to discuss
the values and/or dangers of the mind-blasting produced by drugs,
but I am convinced that the ecstasy for which our human spirits
were made is not produced by cheap artificial methods. It will
come only as our whole beings enter into a union with him whose
sacrificial love is at the center of all things. There will then be no
hangover or withdrawal pains.

Certainly psychology, psychiatry, and the Eastern religions have
much to teach us Christians about the use of our conscious attention.
Douglas Steere tells the story of the Indian student who, after three
years of study with an aged Hindu sage, came one morning as he
was ready to return home. He asked his wise teacher, "Basalmi, I
must now return home. Will you sum up for me your teachings
on the way to enlightenment?" The old man took a piece of bamboo
and wrote one word on the white inside of the bark, *attention*.
The young man was disappointed. "Surely," he cried, "you have
something more to say to me than that!" The old man took the
bark again and wrote another time the same word, *attention*. This
time the student was almost angry, "Surely after three years with
you, there is more you have to say to me of final wisdom than these
two words!" Again the wise old sage took the bamboo and wrote
for the third time, *attention!*

He was summing up the costly experience of the centuries: *The power to put our attention where we choose is the greatest single fact of our human freedom!* In this we are different from rose bushes, grapes, and, so far as we know, all other creatures on this planet. "This is our last great freedom,"[10] says Viktor Frankl, Austrian psychiatrist, in the story of his experience in the Nazi concentration camp during World War II. No matter what happens, however evil or good, terrible or pleasurable the situation is, we still have the freedom to say, "I will" or "I won't." We are free to put our attention where we choose.

This is the freedom which Paul says peculiarly belongs to you who "delight yourselves in God; . . . and never forget the nearness of your Lord" (Phil. 4:4, Phillips). "All that is true, all that is noble, all that is just and pure, all that is lovable and gracious, whatever is excellent and admirable—fill all your thoughts with these things. . . . and the God of peace will be with you" (Phil. 4:8–9, NEB).

"Thought [attention] is the welling up of unknown life into consciousness," writes D. H. Lawrence.

> Thought is gazing on the face of life
> and reading what can be read.
> Thought is pondering over experience
> and coming to conclusion,
> Thought is not an exercise
> or a trick or a set of dodges.
> It is not hearing without listening;
> It is listening and hearing and acting.
> Thought is a man in his wholeness
> wholly attending.[11]

Wholly attending to what? That is the question upon which life, peace, and victory of the spirit depend—or their opposites: our frustration, failure, inadequacy, desperation. Christian prayer is attending to Christ, putting attention on him. "All that came to be was alive with his life, and that life was the light of men. The light shines on in the dark, and the darkness has never quenched it" (John 1:4–5, NEB). "So the Word became flesh and dwelt among us—this Word that was in the beginning with God, the Word that is God, is made flesh and we see his glory full of Grace and truth" (free translation of John 1:1–14).

What kind of attention? Not pleading and begging, but looking with love and adoration, with reverence and awe and with something more—loving reflection and utter openness to see who we are, who our neighbor is, and who God is.

This is the "clear day" in which "you can see forever and ever and evermore." As Evelyn Underhill says so well, "What, in practice, the word adoration implies . . . awe-struck delight in the splendour and beauty of God . . . not a difficult religious exercise but an attitude of the soul."[12]

"But I don't feel like adoring! I certainly don't feel illumined. I see no light, only darkness. Nothing good and worthwhile seems possible to me. I am hostile, afraid, bitter, anxious, frustrated—I feel rotten, sick."

Yes, so do we all at times. That is our common human situation.

"But what do you do then?"

The answer of countless great spirits who have won the victory of faith in every age is: begin where you are. Begin with your discouragement, fear, bitterness, whatever. It isn't where your prayer, meditation, and worship begin but where they end that is important! Begin right where you are now.

How do you get really honest in prayer and worship?

Let me suggest three approaches from my own experience, and from the accumulated experience of countless thousands over the ages.

The first requirement is to be still and *recognize that I am known by God*. There is One in this universe who knows me perfectly, all there is to know about me, *and still values and accepts me*. Now that is a priceless, wondrous discovery, if I am open to it! The illumined words of Psalm 139 (NEB) say it in classic beauty and simplicity.

> Lord, thou hast examined me and knowest me.
> Thou knowest all, whether I sit down or rise up;
>   thou hast discerned my thoughts from afar.
> Thou hast traced my journey and my resting places,
>   and art familiar with all my paths.
> For there is not a word on my tongue
>   but thou, Lord, knowest them all.
> Thou hast kept close guard before me and behind
>   and hast spread thy hand over me.
> Such knowledge is beyond my understanding,
>   so high that I cannot reach it.

> Where can I escape from thy spirit?
> Where can I flee from thy presence?
> If I climb up to heaven, thou art there;
> If I make my bed in Sheol, again I find thee.
> If I take my flight to the frontiers of the morning
>   or dwell at the limit of the western sea,
> even there thy hand will meet me
>   and thy right hand will hold me fast.
> If I say, "Surely darkness will steal over me,
>   night will close around me,"
> darkness is no darkness for thee
>   and night is luminous as day;
> to thee both dark and light are one.

Then the writer really gets honest,

> O God, if only thou wouldst slay the wicked! . . .
> How I hate them, O Lord, that hate thee! . . .
> I hate them with undying hatred.

Now we are getting his true thinking—the way he really feels. But he does not stop there. He goes on with one of the great prayers of all times. "Search me, O God, and know my heart: try me, and know my thoughts: And see if there be any wicked way in me, and lead me in the way everlasting" (Ps. 139:23–24, KJV).

This is the kind of honesty that brings true illumination: to know that I am known by God! He knows me and understands me, even if I don't. If the ancient psalmist could open up his mind and heart, how much more can I open the deepest recesses of my being to God's light. I who have seen revealed the wise loving Father of our Lord Jesus Christ can pray:

> Show me my shell of false values and demands, the deeper hidden compulsions that hide the real me. Reveal to me my heart—your picture of me—not only the false demands to which I have clung, but the true self waiting to be born.

This prayer in contemporary language is similar to the ancient collect for purity.

> Almighty God, unto whom all hearts are open, all desires known,

and from whom no secrets are hid; cleanse the thoughts of our hearts by the inspiration of thy Holy Spirit, that we may perfectly love thee, and worthily magnify thy holy Name; through Christ our Lord. *Amen.*

This has always been our need, to stand in the "clear day" of Christ's light. Then we will begin to see *backward* into the stinking self-centeredness that causes our symptoms of pride, jealousy, greed, lust, fear, and hatred. But we will also look *forward* into the new being that is awaiting us with untold possibilities of giving-love, creative peace, "fortitude and patience with joy." The "clear day" comes when we learn what Jesus meant when he said, "If any man would come after me, let him deny himself ["leave self behind" (NEB)] and take up his cross and follow me" (Mark 8:34, RSV). The clear day came for Saul, the narrow, rigid, bigoted Pharisee, when he met Christ and began to be made over into Paul the apostle of love. "I die every day!" he wrote (1 Cor. 15:31, RSV). "I have been crucified with Christ; it is no longer I who live, but Christ who lives in me" (Gal. 2:20, RSV). The "old man," as Paul, Luther, and Wesley called this false self, has to die—once, twice, yes, daily so that the "new creation in Christ" (2 Cor. 5:17, RSV) may live!

How does this take place? Not by psychology or bootstrapping or do-it-yourself face-lifting, but by opening the self to the light. "You will know the truth, and the truth will make you free," said Jesus (John 8:32, RSV). How often this statement is misquoted. It follows Jesus' declaration of the condition for knowing the deepest and highest truth of all creation. "If you dwell within the revelation I have brought, you are indeed my disciples; you shall know the truth, and the truth will set you free" (John 8:31–32, NEB). Knowing the truth is possible only by adding another clause between the two in this well-known promise of Jesus—a clause necessary if we are to take into account the emphasis of his whole life and teachings. To paraphrase: You shall know the truth and the truth will first make you sick, but when you know that you are sick and need a physician, you may meet the good physician, and the truth he reveals shall set you free. If the Son sets you free, you shall be free indeed (cf. John 8:31–36, Luke 5:31–32).

From Jesus' own experience we get an illustration of what he meant by knowing the truth. Obviously Jesus did not have the "big-shot complex" which was Simon Peter's false picture of himself. But because of Jesus' very humanity, it was necessary for him to spend forty days in the wilderness wrestling with himself and the devil over the difference betwen the current expectations of his people and what the Father's expectations were. He also was struggling with the cost if he accepted that divine will. After the ecstatic experience at his baptism, when he saw further into the nature of Reality than any other man has ever seen, he was given assurance by the Father. "This is my Son, my Beloved, on whom my favor rests" (Matt. 3:17, NEB). Immediately "Jesus was then led away by the spirit into the wilderness, to be tempted by the devil" (Matt. 4:1, NEB).

This, says Douglas Rhymes,

> is that experience of unity with God which was constantly both the joy and the suffering of Christ: it led Him to be driven by the Spirit into the wilderness . . . of the discovery of his real self, tormented by the demons of [what would have been even for Jesus] the false self which will constantly try to hide the real in the superficial: this tormenting and yet important act of self discovery can only be done in solitude.[13]

This is basically true for us all. We too need times of solitude, the wilderness experiences. If it was true for Simon, for Paul, for Wesley, and for our Lord, how much more for you and me. The fact is, as Thomas R. Kelly put it, "No man can look on God and live, live in his own faults, live in the shadow of the least self-deceit."[14]

It is dangerous and costly indeed to look on God in Christ, for it will first make you sick. But only as you continue looking can you become willing to receive the healing and forgiveness that makes you well.

After seeing myself in the light of God's burning, life-giving presence, the second requirement for honesty is *to accept the true and say no to the false*. In God's presence I am able to see the truth and want it so much that I am willing to let go of the false. I am willing to exchange my way for his way! For "what a man is in God's sight, that he is, no more and no less."[15]

However young or old in years, we cannot save ourselves from the false in us. Only in the wondrous love of the eternal Christ can I afford to be honest. Without his acceptance, I could never stand the sight of myself as I really am. But in his presence I can truly overcome my shame and guilt and enter into a clear day where I can see forever and forever and forevermore!

One of our major difficulties in being honest with ourselves is distinguishing between the false self which I must hate and leave behind and the true self which I am to become. Which self is to die and which is to live? Let me share a most helpful illustration. I have used it with many persons—alcoholics with whom I was co-operating in taking the fifth step of the Alcoholics Anonymous program (to admit to God, to myself, and to another person in whom I have confidence the exact nature of my wrongs), persons with marital difficulties, youth and others who were defensively hurting and killing the very things they loved most. I have used it for twenty-five years after receiving the germinal idea for it from a lecture by the Christian psychotherapist, Dr. Fritz Kunkel.

Which life are we to lose and which are we to find? We all want life, but seeking to save the false life means losing the authentic life!

Using the diagram let me seek to make this clear and then follow with some illustrations of the difference between living out of the "heart" and living out of the "shell." (see diagram, p. 107)

Why this description of my false self and my true self is accurate is more easily understood if we realize that each of us has built around himself the shell of a false universe—false desires, phony illusions, silly laws which psychotherapist Dr. Fritz Kunkel calls "training formulaes" carried over from childhood experiences that made me wary and self-deceitful. For instance, "I must have recognition and approval to prove I am not little and unimportant. Not just any old kind of recognition, but the approval I deserve and dream of."

"I must have plenty of money because I must not be poor as I once was. So don't talk to me about mental, spiritual, and cultural riches. These my conscious mind simply will not accept. There is no substitute for plenty of dough!"

"I must have a certain kind of success in my position—perhaps my profession as a doctor, or a clergyman, etc.—not the kind of

KNOWING THE TRUTH ABOUT MYSELF

"If you obey my teaching you are really my disciples: you will know the truth, and the truth will make you free" (John 8:31-32, TEV). "If anyone wants to come with me, . . . he must forget himself, carry his cross, and follow me. For the man who wants to save his own life will lose it; but the man who loses his life for me and for the gospel will save it" (Mark 8:34-35, TEV).

THE SHELL
The Untruth about Me:
My Picture of Myself
What I think I must have to be happy (conscious or unconscious motivations built into my mind by pleasure or pain).
Sin:"I must have this . . . or this . . . or this for life. This is good, isn't it?" My sin is making my picture of good ultimate, preventing me from seeing the true good.

THE HEART
The Truth about Me
God's picture of me — my real potential, the infinite possibilities for my life far greater than I have ever imagined.
Through prayer and worship I am honest with myself before the presence of Christ. I act by faith to deny the false and affirm the true. My shell is broken and I begin.

When my "must-haves" are threatened or attacked, I seek to save myself and

HEART

ACTING OUT OF THE HEART with true wisdom, courage, and love. "The fruit of the Spirit is love, joy, peace, patience, kindness, goodness, faithfulness, gentleness, self-control" (Gal. 5:22, RSV).

ACT OUT OF THE SHELL
blindly, negatively, defensively, foolishly, hurtfully.

SHELL

Three Experiences of Acting by Faith by Which the Spirit Sets Me Free to Live and Act Out of the Heart.

Symptoms of My Sin: Sins resulting from my attempts to save my false self-picture — hostility, rage, fear, suspicion, hatred, foolish worry, mental and emotional exhaustion, physical illness at times, gossip, lying, murder, stealing, fits of passion, misuse of sex, adultery, being overly sensitive, etc.— sins that come from my Sin of trying to play God as I cry, "I must have what I want!"
So in seeking to save my life (my false self), I lose it; that is, my true self—life to the full.

All three are vital parts of valid prayer and worship.
(1) *Insight*: In Christ's presence I have insight, illumination,
   (a) *Into the false*—"My life does not depend on this . . . or this."
   (b)*Into the true*—"This is who I really am!"
(2) *Decision*: I repent, that is, I say no to the false self with its deadly "must-haves" that are not according to reality. I commit, I say yes to the true self so infinitely desirable.
(3) *Trust*: I can and will be my true self in this hour, this day. "I am able." "I have strength for anything through him who who gives me power" (Phil. 4:13, NEB).

The Holy Spirit enters through my honest prayer and commitment to Christ and the Truth.
The Shell is cracked and a large part breaks off. I begin to act out of the heart.
THE NEW CREATION IN CHRIST JESUS IS BEGUN!

success of seeing people made well or set free of injustice, but success based on my own standards or the standards of my peers."

"I must have the presence and help of my wife, my husband, or my child; therefore, I cannot accept the fact of finitude with illness, accidents, and death."

Of course all of these desires are good within themselves, but when we make them ultimate (" 'sin' is a good that is loved inordinately"—Dante), they become our idols or our gods, and they hide and obscure the real good, which I may find even if these demands are never met! So we never see the truth. Our inner compulsions make us literally sick, physically as well as spiritually!

How great the freedom when honestly, openly, frankly, simply I stand in the presence of One who sees me as I am and as I can be. The symbolic illustration on the preceding page indicates what most of us have never realized: we know all about our symptoms, but very little, if anything, about our sin. That is, we are well acquainted with our little sins, though if we are sophisticated, scientifically taught persons, we may not even use the word *sins*. We may refer to them as immaturities, imperfections, weaknesses. But all of us are very conscious of the particular immaturities or habits we know are hurting us and our relations with others, threatening our health and our positions. Therefore, even when we pray, our penitence is not for our sin but for our too quick temper, our foolish worries the doctor says will kill us if we don't quit.

How great the freedom, therefore, when in his presence I see *beyond the symptoms to the sin—the untruth of my conscious and subconscious demands that keeps me in slavery.* My prayers of untruth are wasted breath and time. They get no further than my symptoms and are like rubbing cold cream on the red marks when I have the measles!

"I'm sorry, Lord, that I lost my temper and said such harsh and hurtful things." But deep down in my subconscious my prayer is altogether different. "I was really justified in being so harsh. It was a mean thing he did to threaten my position." Obviously losing my temper in such a situation is not my sin. My sin is the stubborn self-demands that keep me from seeing and doing the best and most constructive things in the situation, even for the enemy—what Jesus meant by "turning the other cheek," "going the second mile."[16]

"Lord, I'm sorry I worry until I'm so exhausted that I am sick and can't sleep. Please take away my worries, forgive my anxieties." Thus I pray consciously, but deep down I am really saying, "I am not at all sorry for idolizing my position. I am determined to protect this self-image at all costs."

"I cannot live without my Mary, my John." Here again worry and excessive grief are not my sins, but rather the demands deep down from my own desires. I am unwilling to trust the Lord of life who, if I cooperate with him, will bring some good even out of the worst. What I need is the honest prayer of self-commitment to the "heart"—God's picture of me at my highest potential of living. This illumination from God's truth and resources gives me courage even when that which I dread the most has come upon me. This is not Pollyanna praying or wishful thinking. It is the realism of a Viktor Frankl in a Nazi concentration camp or a Paul in the Mamertine prison saying, "All joy [in the Lord] be yours. The Lord is near; have no anxiety, but in everything make your requests known to God in prayer and petition with thanksgiving. Then the peace of God, which is beyond our utmost understanding, will keep guard over your hearts and your thoughts, in Christ Jesus" (Phil. 4:4, 6–7, NEB).

On a clear day, in his presence, you can see forever and forever and forevermore! And what you cannot see you can trust, even in the hour of death!

There is a third part of this experience of honesty—a great gift indeed! *In the presence of the living Christ, I see that the truth about me and my world is infinitely better than the half-truths and falsehoods to which I have been clinging.*

This has been the secret of every great and noble person able to be creative and free in the face of danger and seeming failure. It was Dag Hammarskjöld's secret. According to Gustaf Aulén, Hammarskjöld "fought self-centeredness in all its shapes, pursuing it to the deepest and most secret corners: 'So, once again, you chose for yourself.' "[17] This was written in 1955 during one of his attempts as secretary general of the U.N. to bring leaders of the nations together to work for peace.

> So, once again, you chose for yourself—and opened the door to chaos. The chaos you become whenever God's hand does not rest upon your head. . . .

But when his attention is directed beyond and above, how strong he is, with the strength of God who is within him because he is in God. Strong and free, because his false self no longer exists.[18]

"His enemies included the propensity 'furtively to seek honor for yourself,' and 'a tone of voice which places you in the limelight.' 'If you go on in this way, thoughtlessly mirroring yourself in an obituary, you will soon be writing your epitaph—in two senses.' "[19]

Who has not had enough of this experience? Who would not desire to be set free if he really understood the possibilities of freedom? So St. John of the Cross, great Spanish Christian of the last century, wrote his experience.

> Living, and [there is] no life in me?
> [I] languish in expectancy?—
> Dying to my dying day.
>
> Life within me? No, no spark.
> Without God is darkest dark!
> Failing him and failing me
> How can any life but be
> In extremis momently?
> Yearning for my life I say:
> Dying to my dying day!
>
> . . . .
>
> Seeing that what life I know
> Has the face of death to show,
> And that dying's all I do
> Till I come alive in You![20]

Listen to Walter Rauschenbusch (called the Prophet of the Social Awakening) describe the results of illuminating honesty before God. These words have become mine, since I took them at a crisis in my life and ministry, when the little lord self within me had come close to destroying me both physically and spiritually. One day in January, 1947, I entered Rauschenbusch's words in my spiritual diary. I recommend his prayer to each of you as one of the most realistic, hopeful, productive acts in which any human being may engage.

> In the castle of my soul
> Is a little postern gate

Whereat, when I enter,
I am in the presence of God.
In a moment, in the turning of a thought,
I am where God is,
This is a fact.

All life has a meaning,
Without asking I know:
My desires are even now fulfilled,
My fever is gone
In the great quiet of God.
My troubles are but pebbles on the road,
My joys are like the everlasting hills.
. . . .
So it is when my soul steps thru the postern gate
Into the presence of God.
Big things become small, and small things become great.[21]

Yes, thank God, in his presence you have a clear day in which you can see forever, and forever and forevermore.

Therefore when he says to me and to you as he did to Simon Peter, "Lance, John, Mary, Albert, Ruth . . . do you really love me?" I am ready to answer with the ancient psalmist, with Jesus, and Simon, and Paul, Dag Hammarskjöld, St. John of the Cross, and Walter Rauschenbusch: Yes, Lord, "search me, . . . and know my heart: try me, and know my thoughts: . . . and lead me in the way everlasting" (Ps. 139:23–24).

NOTES

1. Thomas E. Clarke, S.J., "Can Man Encounter God Today?" in Mooney, *Prayer: The Problem of Dialogue with God*, p. 14.
2. See the story of his dispute with Paul in Gal. 1–2.
3. David M. Stanley, S.J., "Contemplation of the Gospels," in Mooney, p. 55.
4. Ibid., p. 73. The last italics are mine.
5. Ibid., pp. 56–57.
6. Ibid.
7. Frederick W. Faber, "There's a Wideness in God's Mercy."
8. Alfred Lord Tennyson, "The Higher Pantheism."
9. Copyright © 1965 by Alan Jay Lerner and Burton Lane. Used by permission of Chappell & Co., Inc.

10. Viktor E. Frankl, *Man's Search for Meaning* (Boston: Beacon Press, 1959).

11. D. H. Lawrence, *Last Poems.*

12. Evelyn Underhill, *The Spiritual Life* (New York: Harper & Row, 1936,), p. 61.

13. Douglas Rhymes, *Prayer in the Secular City* (Philadelphia: Westminster Press, 1967), pp. 31–32.

14. Thomas R. Kelley, *A Testament of Devotion* (New York: Harper & Bros., 1941), p. 65.

15. Thomas à Kempis, *The Imitation of Christ.*

16. See Lance Webb, *The Art of Personal Prayer* (Nashville: Abingdon Press, 1962), pp. 25–43.

17. Aulén, *Dag Hammarskjold's White Book,* p. 80.

18. Hammarskjöld, *Markings,* p. 104.

19. Aulén, p. 80.

20. From *The Poems of St. John of the Cross,* Original Spanish Texts, and New English Versions by John Frederick Nims. Published by Grove Press, Inc. © 1959 by John Frederick Nims, p. 31.

21. "The Little Gate to God" ("The Postern Gate") from *Walter Rauschenbusch* by Dores Robinson Sharpe. © 1942, by The Macmillan Company.

5 The
New Song
of Acceptance

The Joy and Freedom of Being Accepted and of Accepting

There is indeed no greater joy on earth than the freedom of new perspective and illumination which comes when I consciously recognize myself through authentic prayer and worship as being in the presence of God the Reality we meet in Christ!

It is the freedom of coming out of the shell of the false must-haves and the joy of becoming more and more the true person that has been potential in me all along! For now I no longer struggle along false battle lines.

I do not have to have my false, twisted picture of life fulfilled! Indeed I no longer want it fulfilled, but rather hate it as my worst enemy!

As much as I desire the presence and health of my dearest loved ones and my own physical health, I no longer feel that without these I cannot be truly alive!

My old demands look as foolish as they always were, but now I see them for what they are!

I have no compulsive need to be recognized, to be popular, to be strong physically!

I no longer demand proof. I do not have to see and understand all the mysteries of good and evil. Like Job, I cease to ask why with such passionate vehemence. Rather, I ask only how? Show me. Lead me.

I can trust myself because I am trusted beyond what I deserve!

I can trust others even though I am aware of the wrong they have done or plan to do. In this trust in God and his purposes for us all, I can do the appropriate best thing for all in the situation.

I can love even those I do not like, for I trust eternal Love.

All of this is possible because I can accept what God is giving me—the priceless gift of freedom to be my authentic self.

I do not have to struggle to make myself infinitely wise, perfectly secure, but I can accept my finitude, my limitations of knowledge and strength. I know more of who I am and can be in God's sight, and the view is more wonderful than any I had imagined before.

As some of you read this, you may be tempted to shake your head or your fist! The sad and tragic fact is that so often we are lacking in this most significant insight that makes life worth living and pain and death worth meeting! How few clear days in which we can see a little way down our misty path much less forever and ever! "Perhaps," you may say to me, "you are indulging in a romantic fantasy. It is poetic, but unrealistic."

My answer is, "No, I am utterly serious when I say from my own experience that when we lack this illumination and its freedom, we are prevented from accepting God's most priceless gift—life at its fullest and best."

It is difficult to be a real Christian today or even a person of good will and integrity. There are so many pressures and tensions, ambiguities of moral standards in a world where future shock is upon us and we are unprepared. We live in a world that is not unmoral so much as amoral—a secular culture where there is a deep credibility gap between worship and work, belief and practice, a gap so deep many do not even see it.

Why are prayer and worship being abandoned by so many people? It is not primarily because of antiquated forms of worship, though improving the forms in order that they may be more readily and helpfully used is important. The needed reforms of our liturgy have made matters worse for some. "Beforehand for most people the problem was dormant: the antiquated and unsatisfactory forms of worship at least had an aura of venerable tradition. Now the reforms have created an expectation they cannot fulfill and have left people constantly irritated by the grating inadequacy of . . . worship."[1] Why this irritation and abandonment of prayer and worship? Professor Davis makes clear his own answer.

> I am not saying that we Christians today should no longer believe and worship. I am saying that our faith and worship are not part

of its socially shared and confirmed reality. As believers and worshippers we step outside the dominant secular culture as social deviants. . . . The world of faith no longer has that accent of reality which is given by the confirmation and approval of society as a whole. In our culture faith and all that faith talks about are surrounded by an air of unreality. . . . It was not so in a Christian culture.[2]

As "social deviants" from our culture, many honest persons find prayer and worship both intellectually and emotionally dishonest.

Mr. Davis sees only two alternatives—the ghetto or the desert. By the *ghetto,* he means renouncing the secular world and building a subculture as the Jews, the Amish, and other Protestant and Roman Catholic groups have done which isolates them from the world in which they live. This he rejects, for God has given us the secular world. To deny the many good things in it would be denying God's gift. By the *desert,* he means continuing to live in the secular world but going into the underground church for worship and fellowship, prayer and meditation. This was necessary for Davis because for him the institutional church has become too much identified with the secular culture surrounding it. Happily the other thirty-five participants in this consultation representing the major bodies of Christendom around the world rejected these as the only alternatives. Most of them saw another possibility—belonging to the *communitas* of loving and committed brothers in the family of God which may be, and often is, in the institutional church. We may live in a communitas that takes seriously the need for disciplined use of time and attention, so that each of its members is supported by a community of those who have found perspective and illumination for life at its best. Thus they are able to accept the gifts of God with intellectual and emotional honesty.

A supportive fellowship of acceptance and understanding is of first importance if we are to understand and obey the law of love. Only as new creations in Christ can we obey the positive demands of Christlike love in a world of wars. Our inability to meet these conflicts with love leads to addictions to drugs, alcohol, tobacco, and other favorite insanities. Seward Hiltner in a helpful book *Ferment in the Ministry* speaks of our ATC level (Ambiguity, Tension Capacity) in the midst of such a confused, ambiguous, contradictory, and uncertain quest for life. Each person has the ability to stand only so much contradiction with his own desire for order and meaning. When these contradictions are added to the pressures that seek to force us to change our ways and tempt us to give up and quit, our ATC level may be much lower than required for balanced, creative living. When this happens, we may go under.

Hiltner's book deals mainly with the ordained minister in the institutional church. An increasing number of clergymen are finding their ATC levels at a very low ebb, but so are many people in other spheres of life. For instance, I know personally several parents who are attempting to be effective Christian mothers and fathers. They want to love their children rather than smother them. They also want to bring them up with a positive, intelligent faith which will result in a mature life. But they are overwhelmed with the crowding responsibilities of their vocation and of their environment. They rightly fear that their children's peer group will be stronger than their own family's faith and teaching! False and trusted values exalted in the sixteen to eighteen thousand hours of television the average seventeen-year-old youth will see—plus the twelve thousand hours of public school and the thousands of other hours with companions at play with an almost total secular emphasis—may be difficult to counteract.[3]

The secular world teaches the opposite of what the church teaches during two or three hours of worship and church school on Sunday. "Money talks." "Selfishness pays." "Self-giving love is weakness and therefore foolish." "Bearing a cross for others is folly!" Obviously there are vital Christian parents who spend many hours each week in the nurture of their children to supplement the Christian nurture of the larger church, but this is the rare exception. Even when it is done, sometimes the peer group and other influences are still greater than that of the home.

One of the saddest stories I know is one that in general outline could be duplicated many times. It happened in a family where the father and mother are brilliant, well-educated, mature persons. They had given as much time as they could to be with their children—on vacations, weekends, in table talk, and at other times. Under pressures of going into the army or becoming a conscientious objector, the son finally decided to enlist. He had to face the constant inner conflict of his repugnance of killing. He was derided by his buddies and his officers for being "weak" and "sissy." On the day he was to ship out for Vietnam, he could stand the conflict no longer and tried to take his own life. Fortunately he was found in time, put in the hospital, and given medical discharge. There followed several months of depression. The load on his parents was almost unbearable. The mother, in spite of her Christian faith and training, found her ATC level inadequate and became ill. Both she and her husband came through it as they found a new perspective and strength in the privilege of being accepted and of accepting.

This is one story that has the possibility of a good ending for all. I know several other family situations where the youth have left home and joined hippie colonies[4] or who have swelled the ranks of the drifters as James Michener calls them.[5] The ATC conflict for youth is often truly unbearable. Drug addiction and wasted years are threatening to destroy them. Indeed, in some cases the worst has happened. I know some parents whose ATC level could not take it. They have cracked up in bitterness and despair. Their Christian faith was too superficial to lead them to the peace and perspective of acceptance by God, themselves, and their deviant children. When opportunities came to help their rebellious children, they were unable to accept them and the situation worsened.

Charles Davis is right. As Christians we are "social deviants" in a secular culture. For this reason the ATC level of a concerned parent, father, husband, wife, business or professional man, teacher, youth, or a person of any other human situation may be, and often is, dangerously low. Whatever else the secular world of scientific technology may have to offer, it does not have much, if anything, to say about the ambiguities of human life. The tensions between our human "must-haves" and the realities of our situation are entirely too strong for us to meet and overcome them with only the resources of secular man. So if my ATC level is low, it is for two reasons: as a professing Christian I am a social deviant in a pagan, secular culture; and I have not learned to discipline my life in the faith I profess in the presence and love of the eternal Christ!

I am very sure, therefore, that none of us is ready for life in this secular world as mature persons—the end result of living as vital Christians—until we learn the gracious privilege of being accepted with all our failures and weaknesses. We will never know the overflowing, lovingly creative life until and unless we have learned to sink our roots into the flowing streams of God's grace. This can happen only through a disciplined life of prayer and worship, through intelligent, honest thinking and through devotion and openness before God. This kind of disciplined life produces what I am calling the third great stream of living water: *acceptance*—acceptance of the perspectives that illumine us as to who we are and what life can be in the light of who God is.

In these disciplines we also accept our daily bread—forgiveness, reconciliation with God and man, and guidance and deliverance. All of these are summed up in the last half of the Lord's Prayer. "Father, . . . Give us day by day the food we need. Forgive us our sins, for we forgive everyone who has done us wrong. And do not bring us to hard testing" (Luke 11:3-4, TEV). Only when we have learned to pray this and live as we pray will our ATC level be high enough to live effectively in this secular world!

The tragic fact is that the meaning of vital Christian prayer and worship, even in the songs and hymns and in the other habits of devotion that once went under the name of Christian piety, is little understood and practiced today. This is because of their false and harmful use. Michener, describing the brilliant and idealistic youth who as drifters were escaping from life and its responsibilities, says this about their religious faith.

> The second surprising aspect of religion. It was rarely mentioned. Occasionally Cato referred to his hatred of what Christianity had done to the Negro, but he was speaking sociologically; Yigal sometimes spoke of the problems faced by the Jews in Israel, but only their political problems, never their theological. I would go for a month without hearing God mentioned, not even as a curse word. With this generation He had become an expletive, used primarily by girls, as when Monica or Britta cried, "My God, look!" He was used to draw attention to camels or especially beautiful mosques, but His ancient relationship to eschatology or morality was not referred to. I think if some college girl from our midwest, sitting on the bed at Inger's, had asked, "Do you believe in God?" the crowd would have passed out stone-cold, as if hit by an extra strong cookie. About half the young people, especially those from Australia and Canada, were Catholic, but they were as indifferent as the others.[6]

Millions who still profess Christian belief, even some ordained pastors, have quit praying except as a last resort. Then they may turn to the unknown God who *might* be there!

Secular man exhibits three distinct attitudes toward prayer. The first is the childish, "Gimme." "Help me get what I want." When there is a need, beg God and he will come running. Bishop A. T. Robinson refers to this as prayer to "the God of the gaps"; but the gaps are mostly closed. For example, much of the time we no longer need God when we are sick, for there is penicillin or surgery, the doctor and medicine! And for protection, we have safety belts and common sense. What more does a liberated man or woman need?

The second attitude toward prayer is on the adolescent level—*not* praying. Realizing how foolish our childish praying was, we give up all prayer as unscientific, superstitious magic. This abandonment of prayer is nothing new. Before all this talk of secular man, Mark Twain's Huckleberry Finn was thoroughly secularized. Read his confession:

> Miss Watson she took me in the closet and prayed, but nothing came of it. She told me to pray every day, and whatever I asked for I would get it. But it warn't so. I tried it. Once I got a fishline, but no hooks. I tried for the hooks three or four times, but somehow I couldn't make it work. By and by, one day, I asked Miss Watson to try for me, but she said I was a fool. She never told me why, and I couldn't make it out no way. I set down one time back in the woods, and had a long think about it. I says to myself, if a body can get anything they pray for, why don't Deacon Winn get back the money he lost on pork? Why can't the widow get back her silver snuffbox that was stole? Why can't Miss Watson fat up? No, says I to myself, there ain't nothin' to it.

Many "scientific" minded persons in our secular age have reached this simplistic conclusion.

Some, however, have advanced to a third level which is somewhat beyond complete skepticism: either a humanistic prayer of psychological adjustment that brings "peace of mind" or the view of prayer as simply social action—to do good is to pray. The best prayer is actually going out to remove injustice, to meet great needs, to heal and to restore the hurt and the wounded. Certainly this is the highest level of purely secular prayer and much to be preferred to either of the other attitudes. The chief difficulty, and to my mind and experience, an insufferable one, is that I go out as one, little, self-sufficient person, joining others who have the same ideals, but without the perspectives of who we are or why we should care.

With this approach we have no deep roots that can supply us with the proper insights, the necessary patience, and above all, the love needed when the going is rough. For our concerned action *is* going to be rebuffed and unappreciated. If we continue, we will be faced with the cross or its equivalent. Then, as countless persons have done, we may give up our idealism and seek to escape. Or we may join the anarchists who would blindly destroy what they cannot change. As self-sufficient persons depending solely on our own resources and the help of our fellows, our "prayer of action" is soon likely to be empty and then discarded as the way gets rougher.

The fact is that on any of these three levels we lose the deep meaning and power of Christian prayer: the *perspective* that brings *illumination* that leads to *acceptance* and *caring involvement*.

These are all key words to describe the life-giving results of praying in a genuinely Christlike manner. When we tap the living water of *acceptance,* several valuable experiences result.

We find the *wisdom* and *courage* to accept "the food we need for today" which includes not only a *sense of purpose,* but the health and strength of mind and body to fulfill it.

We accept ourselves as forgiven so that we no longer need carry with us the burden of guilt over past failures and sins. This means also that because we "accept our acceptance" in the forgiving love of God, we can accept and forgive ourselves—and that is one of the hardest of all accomplishments. Then and then only can we truly *forgive others.*

Still another part of this "bread for today" is the acceptance of the *guidance* we so greatly need in order to make choices leading to the good in even the worst times.

Thus we can accept the *deliverance* from the evils and temptations that threaten to test us beyond our ability to overcome or to endure.

As we think of each of these kinds of acceptance that mark Christian prayer at its authentic best, it is obvious that each has been associated too often with what might be called "magical hocus-pocus"—or just plain superstition! However, the true meaning of forgiveness, guidance, and deliverance for one who has at last said no to the false life and yes to the true life as the Spirit reveals it is not superstition but the most intelligent realism! For it will bring life over death, hope out of despair, joy out of sadness, and love over hate. To understand these meanings let us consider each of these four last phrases of the prayer of Jesus.

Give us this day our daily bread.
It is obvious, or ought to be, that before we can give bread to others we must be fed. We must first accept our own creatureliness, recognizing our humble dependence not only on our fellow-man but primarily on the Source and Giver of life. "He is," says Jacopone de Todi, "the grand donatore, Pastor and Pasture of the soul."

In these days of travel to the moon, we recognize how completely we depend on each other and even more on the rich resources and laws of our physical and personal universe. So with faith we pray, "Give us this day our daily bread."

To pray thus is not to beg but to accept. God the Father to whom Jesus prayed does not want beggars but sons. Beggars wheedle and whimper. Sons ask and receive, according to their deepest needs. Artists have painted different kinds of praying hands. Albrecht Dürer painted uplifted hands of adoration and blessing. Another artist painted open hands receiving gifts from the Father of life. Both pictures are valid: hands that express the living adoration of reverence, yielded, submitting to a greater wisdom and love than ours, and also hands that express the open receptiveness of trusting hearts that eagerly receive all the Father has to give. "Ask, seek, knock, and you *will* receive" was Jesus' admonition (Luke 11: 9–10). But ask not as abject worms in the dust, cowering slaves before a hard master. No, you are to ask, seek, and knock with persistence as sons of the Father who knows your needs better than you know them. Unworthy? Yes, but made worthy by being called to the life of sons. (See Gal. 4:6–7.)

Jesus taught us to ask for and accept "the bread for today's needs and when tomorrow comes, there will be bread enough for that day too!"

God's bread is mostly plain bread—not some purely spiritual substance for ethereal souls, but substantial bread for the whole persons which we are. We can, under some circumstances, live for days without physical bread, but our fullest life comes when we have bread for all our needs, physical, mental, and spiritual, including our brothers' needs as well. Indeed, it is bread for our common life, its toils and trials, its joy and laughter, its griefs and troubles, its hurts and surprises, including each painful step of self-knowledge, every opportunity to love and to give. In all of these God's bread is given and those who accept are fed! Surely this is what Jesus meant when he said, "I am the bread of life, he that eats of the bread I shall give him shall never hunger, and he that drinks of the water I shall give him shall never thirst!"

Lest these words be dismissed as abstract and ethereal, let me illustrate the difference Christian prayer and worship as the acceptance of that bread and water of life make. Such acceptance is the opposite of the proud rejection of the equally proud taking by force what I want. It is acceptance in trust of the vision and strength, the hope and help needed for this day and all the days to come, not for ourselves only but for everyone else as well.

My daughter Jeanne has given me the privilege of sharing her recent experiences as at age thirty-six she found herself literally starving to death for this "plain bread of life." This was true even though she had grown up in a Christian home and church where she had been taught since infancy the meanings of the Christian faith. Those who know her will agree with me that she is an unusually gifted person. She has a superb soprano voice, is an excellent organist, pianist, and choral director. She is a good thinker and teacher with a striking, lovable personality. She can describe the Christian way interestingly and convincingly. Let me quote directly from her own account of the crisis in which she began to take "bread for daily needs," as she had never been able to do before.

"For most of my thirty-six years God's living presence has been very real in my life. There have been dry spells of months in which I have felt very alienated from him. Each time this has happened my return has been a marvelously joyous experience.

"Finally this winter I discovered the source of these periods of alienation. I have conscientiously and caringly tried to do 'God's will,' to be the person he wanted me to be, to use to the full *all* the gifts he has given me.

"Most of the time, it seemed fairly obvious what he would have me do; and I seemed to be extremely successsful in carrying out these goals. I worked hard and was never satisfied until I had given my best to achieve success. All the while my self-confidence was blossoming, and I felt that undoubtedly I could accomplish *well* whatever *I* might set out to do.

"At thirty I found myself to be quite capable in a number of areas—musician, speaker, youth leader, teacher, actress, cook, seamstress—and I was working very hard at being a good wife and mother (although these latter were the hardest jobs of all).

"As these next years progressed, the instant successes I had known became much harder to achieve and life wasn't handing out the bouquets I was used to. The dry spells were more frequent, and I became a very angry young woman, fighting myself and the circumstances of my life. I was furious because it was so increasingly evident that I was *not* fulfilling my own plan of life which I identified as 'God's plans' for me.

"There was so much to do and I was so very tired all the time. It seemed that I couldn't please *anyone* any more. *Nothing* went right. I loved my children and my husband *so much,* and I couldn't imagine for a minute living without them, yet it seemed they were driving me crazy.

"Here I was the 'Great Jeanne'—the modern success story capable of such exciting things—struggling to take care of a huge house that only got dirty again the minute it was cleaned, facing an endless succession of meals to cook, dishes to wash, crying, fighting children, and husband with needs and a ministry to be shared. Yes, I was involved in music and youth and teaching, but so very little of it was even *touching* the resources I felt were stored within me. *I was failing God and everyone, and I was furious and sick—physically and spiritually sick.*"

Obviously the crisis came to her, as it does to many of us, when she painfully realized that she could not do both her music and her home in the perfect way she wanted to do them. She was torn between her responsibilities as mother and wife and her desires for self-fulfillment as a musician. Her "must-haves" were tearing her apart even while she continued praying and asking God for help. While she rebelled at her impossible situation, it became worse. Let her describe the result which could have been tragic indeed without her discovery of the deeper meanings of the kind of prayer her faith required.

"Finally, one bleak midwinter day, I faced the fact that I was heading straight into physical and emotional disaster. All the strong will power and self-sufficiency and even my prayers to God for strength were not going to pull me through this time! I had reached the very *bottom* of my *own* resources. [The first requirement for the prayer of faith is this recognition that no one is ever self-sufficient in his own resources. The *bottom* is the place to begin whether it is Jeanne and her demand for perfection, or an alcoholic's or any other kind of self demands.] I had never been here before. In desperation I was reading some devotional material. Here were the words I had heard so often and had always found to be distasteful: *'submit'*—'Submit *all* your life! *All your plans!* And *then accept life as it comes!'*

"I had rejected this approach before because it had always seemed to be a *cop out!* It appeared to be just a good excuse to give up! Surely, I felt, God expects more of me! And so with *my* strong will I had never really completely submitted myself to God's will. [Like the alcoholic salesmanager, she was trying to *use* God to help her achieve the plans of the "Great Jeanne!"]

"Now at last I was ready. I really had no choice, except going under completely.

"For several months I had been using the guitar for fun as accompaniment for informal occasions and to teach old and new folk songs to the youth in my church. On this day of my saying yes to God's will for me, whatever it might involve, I wrote some new words to the old Negro spiritual, 'Lonesome Valley.' I knew from experience the truth of the first two stanzas.

> Jesus walked this lonesome valley
> He had to walk it for himself.
> Nobody else could walk it for him,
> He had to walk it for himself.

> I must go and face my trials
> Gotta face them for myself.
> Nobody else can face them for me.
> Gotta face them for myself.

Now as a means to my acceptance and commitment I added two more.

There is hope within my valley.
There is hope for my despair.
No more alone within my valley.
Jesus is with me and he cares.

Jesus I submit my future
With its worries and its fears.
Now as I walk along my valley
Hope for new life and strength appears.
Now Jesus walks beside me here.

"One result of my complete submission to God was that I began to find the insights I so desperately needed—the 'third viewpoint!' I looked at my life from God's perspective and was amazed to see so many meaningful, exciting ways to use my talents. Actually I had been aware of many of these possibilities before but had impatiently rejected them because they seemed inferior to the 'great' plans I knew God had for me.

"Now I see that these 'great' plans in and of themselves are quite shallow. Someday, I may yet carry out some of these ideas, but how much more exciting it is to live fully and wholly in the real world in which I actually find myself today.

"I couldn't face this real world before but am beginning to do so now that I have accepted the courage and peace, the deliverance as the gift of God in this new relationship."

Jeanne began to walk in her new life of submission and acceptance of herself, her family, her musical gifts, and her ability to lead others. She told me of another incident on one of the days that followed. She was discovering to her surprise and delight the best ways to combine these seemingly conflicting needs into a creative life.

On this particular day, things seemed to be more confused than usual. Her two noisy children were fighting and demanding her attention. It was the same old problem as before, but now she found in the middle of it all the ability to see and accept her life in new perspective. During this day she wrote some significant lines describing her new life. She did it in between ministering to crying children, stopping to bind up a wound, breaking up a fight, preparing a meal, and practicing the solo she was to sing the next day. These lines describe better than any words of mine the meaning

of Jesus' promise in suggesting that we pray "Give us our bread for
this day's needs."

> *What is Life?*
> It is the process of being hurt and of hurting.
> of forgiving and of being forgiven.
> of loving and of being loved.
> It contains much pain and frustration.
> It seems impossible. . . .
> It contains God
> and the grace of his presence.
> It contains victory
> and an absurd triumph over all odds
> and against all reason.
> It continues to wring and twist our private little
> hopes and dreams
> until they are ragged, torn and meaningless.
> Finally, when all seems wrecked and beyond repair,
> it throws us into a *new perspective*
> and a *new vision.* . . .
>   IF
> We have eyes to see.
> (If we cannot see, then there is no more life . . .
> *We are dead* . . .
> even if our bodies continue to function
> for awhile longer.)
> Side by side with disaster then life brings
> peace
> and
> an unbelievable strength. . . .
> I submit myself, O God to life . . .
> to the *life* you give.

Commenting on her new freedom and strength, she wrote, "This
was what my new life was all about. The disaster was gone. The
same situations were present, but I had a whole new creative approach. I found new ways of using my talents and a perspective
on what I was already doing that transformed everything.

"Like an alcoholic, I still must live one day at a time and *resubmit*
myself when the days are particularly trying."

Here we have it, and we are all indebted to Jeanne for this good
description of the glorious acceptance that comes from complete

submission to the loving will of God in Christ! She learned as we must learn that *she could not receive unless she were willing to give,* and not under her conditions but his. She learned to pray, "Our Father . . . your will be done. . . . Give us day by day the food we need."

Notice that it is *"Our Father"* to whom we pray, "Give *us* our daily bread." She, like so many of us who have prayed the Lord's Prayer all our lives, had prayed too often for *"my* bread, the right and power to fulfill myself." "Surely this is *'my* right,' is it not, to do *my* thing?" But if we pray in truth we soon discover that *"my* thing" is really *"our* thing" and the ability to fulfill *myself* comes as I submit my self-fulfillment to the larger fulfillment of his way for all who are involved in my situation. For all of us, like Jeanne, are related to others.

Indeed the whole tenor of Jesus' life and teaching indicates his conviction that anyone who is not interested in and involved with others in a concern for their daily bread cannot accept the bread he himself needs. "I was hungered and you gave me no meat. Depart from me; I never knew you."

Indeed, God's bread is given to us in large bundles, too much for our own consumption alone. If we try to keep it for ourselves, we get fat and sick, as happens to so many Americans today, physically and spiritually. This approach to *"my* bread" leads to boredom, hatred, and wrong relationships with others.

For instance, it is tragic when an ordained minister loses "his bread"—his acceptance of the purpose God has for him and his submission to the greater good—because he is so desperately concerned to get his own self-fulfillment, to find his place and position, to be recognized. As a result, when the people come to worship, they look up and are not fed. It is equally tragic for parents and other adults to give their children "a stone when they ask for bread or a serpent when they ask for fish," as Jesus put it. If they don't have any bread for themselves, how can they give it to their children? Like Jeanne, they may have the words of the Good News, but they have not accepted the relationship that would enable them to be free, creative, and loving. We cannot give the bread of life to anyone else when we haven't accepted it and, like Jeanne, are literally starving to death for lack of it.

This is not only true in our family relationships, but in our wider relationships in the church, in the communities, and in the world where we live. We will certainly lose our own bread if we continue unconcerned with bread for all of the children of God—in East St. Louis, in Peoria, in Chicago, in Mississippi, in South America, in India, or wherever they starve physically or spiritually. This is an immutable law of our human relatedness. We are economically as well as geographically and spiritually *one* people—God's children, and we all need bread. *Give us this day our daily bread.*

Forgive us as we forgive those who have wronged us.
Christian prayer and worship are *the acceptance of forgiveness with the corresponding ability to forgive others.* Indeed we cannot accept ourselves as forgiven unless we accept others and forgive them. This is also an immutable law of personal health and life.

Here again forgiveness of both kinds is the acceptance of a gift. We cannot with our own limited abilities correct the disorder and heal the hurts, hates, and selfishness or bridge the gaps cut in the tender flesh of our own hearts or of our families, our cities, our nation, and our world. When I am hurt and stepped on, my security and rights threatened or removed, and I stand alone facing the world as my enemy, I can do one of three things.

I can give up and cravenly crawl into my shell of bitterness, protecting myself as best I can while I hide, hate, and finally die. Many people choose this way as various kinds of mental illness attest, including addiction to drugs, alcohol, money, or a craving for power.

One of the most intelligent young women I have known in recent years took this way of escape. She was reacting to her feelings of insecurity brought about by being ridiculed as a child. Because she was overweight, the boys did not pay attention to her, she thought, as much as they did some of the small, cute girls. Also as an only child with a busy mother, when she returned home from school, she was often alone. Though her mother and father were active in the church and "salt of the earth" types of loving, dependable persons, evidently she felt they had not really cared for her. She began to withdraw into her shell and to compensate with daydreams and fantasies. At the age of fifteen her need for acceptance and her bitterness toward her parents, toward God, and toward the "square" world that had hurt her led her to fall in with a man of low character. He persuaded her to leave home and go with him. He also introduced her to drugs and alcohol. In spite of all her parents could do during the months preceding and after this desperate act of hiding from life, she continued with the man until he abandoned her. From one sordid and pathetic attempt after another to find acceptance among those who took advantage of her, she came at last back to the city where her parents lived. Still she refused to have anything to do with them except in times of extreme need. Her parents went the second mile many times to accept her, including helping her with an unexpected baby. Their forgiving love and the coming of the child whom she chose to keep are beginning to work a miracle in her spirit, though at this writing she still has a long way to go. As I think of her I wonder what would have happened to her had she been like many other young people whose parents foolishly believe that the provision for their child's material needs is a substitute for giving-love or have been divorced and left the youth feeling rejected and alone.

We know the answer, of course, for our correctional institutions are full of them. Some, like the sheep of the story in the last chapter, go on over the precipice to a tragic ending.[7]

If I do not withdraw and escape from the rejections and indignities that come to me, I may strike out at others in revenge. To get out my hostilities may be healthier for me at the moment, but to do so as a way of life creates a growing circle of hatred and hostilities. Every youth who leaves home because of lack of acceptance does so partially to get revenge on those who may really care for him. If the feeling of being unwanted and "put down" is strong enough, the youth may actually enter upon a life of crime in order to vent his hostilities on his family, his teachers, and the uncaring world!

This motive of "standing up for my rights," "getting even," "showing them I'm not the inferior person they think I am" is the basis for *personal* wars of every kind. In the same manner group or racial feelings of insecurity and inferiority result in class, racial, and national wars. The rapid growth of the Nazi party, shown so vividly in the recent account *The Rise of the Third Reich* by William Shirer, is certainly traceable to this revenge—"We'll show the rest of the world what a great people we are." This is surely the mood of many black and white militants who desire revenge more than reconstruction. But though our hatred is turned toward great evils and injustices, the way of hostility and revenge is in the end more destructive than constructive. Like Don Quixote, with righteous feelings we go out fighting windmills of evil and attacking the injustices about us, but without the spirit of Christlike love, we return with our own sword of life bruised and broken.

A minister may preach "prophetic sermons" in the name of fighting evils. But when these messages express more of the hostilities of the preacher than his genuine concern for the hurts of others, they will always fail. As Dr. Tom Bennett, psychologist and management counselor, warned a group of pastors recently, "When the preacher identifies his own hurts with the evils he sees in others and goes out to 'blast 'em,' he may get something off his chest, but he is also likely to find his ministry useless and damaging." So also for the person in any sphere who perpetually "blasts 'em" and "tells them off."

The unforgiving, merciless spirit, no matter whether in parent, teacher, pastor, bishop, reformer, or just plain citizen, cannot bring the healing, reconciling spirit of Christ into any situation. This is true no matter how just the cause or how unjust the evils that are attacked. This merciless spirit is the source of the unrecognized but potent anarchy, right or left, in those who would destroy the church or the state or the university or the home because they have been hurt by the system or by some authority figure in it. Those who cannot forgive cannot believe in the possibilities of the slow workings of democracy, which is the dependence on free people making the right decisions with adequate teaching and leadership. Rebellions on college and university campuses, antiwar crusades, church-renewal battlers, the crusaders against rigidities in public education— all of these often have real injustices and evils to attack; but in this spirit their tactics are often in the end self-defeating. The fight against wrongs and injustice should never be abandoned; but without forgiving acceptance the only possibility is to destroy the enemy, even if it means destroying oneself and, like ancient Samson, pulling the temple down not only on our own heads but on everybody around us! This blind revolution ends in nihilism. It is a million miles away from anything constructive, from any kind of creative revolution that embraces the hurt and wounded, that works effectively with others for changes to prevent the continuation of the injustice.

Then there is the *way of forgiveness.* The young girl rejected by her peers and her parents may now accept them even as she is accepted. Instead of destroying the enemy, I am ready to treat him as a friend, not giving up or over to his evil, but in many cases breaking down the walls between us and helping him to work with me for good. Even when this happy reconciliation is rejected by the other person, I am still able to accept the suffering involved without bitterness! This truth holds good in group as well as personal situations. Sometimes I cannot change it myself. If my witness in opposition to the evils, however costly, is to be constructive, it will require a genuinely forgiving approach.

Another fact needs to be recognized. *He who does not accept himself as forgiven cannot forgive, and he who does not forgive cannot accept himself as forgiven!* This impasse can be met only by the love of Christ who forgives us before we ask him. No matter how we fight and struggle with all the hurt we do for ourselves and others, he never treats us as his enemy! He may let me suffer the results of my sin, but he always goes with me to the "pig pen" where I find myself hungry and forsaken; and, when I let him, he forgives and leads me back to life! Consider the words of Jesus to the poor, bitter paralytic, blaming and hating God and himself for his illness, as he was let down from the roof top in the presence of Jesus. "Your sins are forgiven. . . . Rise, take up your bed and go home" (Matt. 9:2, 7, RSV).

Or consider the soldiers and the mob who took out their hostilities toward life and others on the innocent and loving Jesus as they nailed him to the cross. Neither had they asked for forgiveness, but they heard his words spoken from the depths of his own suffering, "Father, forgive them; for they know not what they do" (Luke 23:34, RSV).

This gift is what John Wesley and others have called "prevenient grace"—God's gracious love that is there for me before I ask for it! But to be mine and to be given to others, I must accept it.

The precious gift of God's acceptance and forgiveness enabling me to accept and to forgive myself has been given to me over and over in the crisis times when my self-assurance and self-dependence were badly shaken. Suddenly seeing oneself as self-centered and hurting one's own loved ones through self-centeredness is the costliest of all revelations! No doubt it is one of the bitterest pills anyone is called to take. Perhaps it is even more costly than seeing and accepting one's hurtful failures and immaturities in one's own vocation or social life. Many times I have needed desperately the medicine of self-acceptance and forgiveness in both worlds.

One morning I came down to breakfast after having spent several late hours the night before with the family of a young man who had just been killed in an auto accident. The ministry of comfort and hope is never easy in such a time. The family appreciated my presence. They seemed to receive help from my prayer as I left them in the presence of the mystery of their young son's tragic death. I had not tried to *give* them *the answers* because I never claimed to have them. I did seek to leave them "held by the eternal Love" who would see them through. I went home and to bed, exhausted and sad because the lad was dear also to me.

Next morning at breakfast I was very weary. Instead of being thankful for my opportunities, I was feeling sorry for myself. At least this was my best justification for my actions as I tried to explain them to myself later. At the table I was impatient when my twin daughters, age twelve, were noisy and fussy. I spoke roughly to them. "Why didn't they appreciate my 'great efforts' of the night before and cease their quarreling?" I asked myself. But they had their own problems, and a few minutes later we rushed to get in the car so I could take them to school on the way to my study. As we drove along, Ruth, wiping away her tears, looked up and asked, "Dad, sometimes your prayers don't mean very much do they?" She was referring to the morning devotions at the table, and I knew exactly what she meant. Her words went like an arrow to my heart. I answered as bravely as I could, "You are right, Ruthie. This morning I was unkind and thoughtless. Even though I had a bad night and was weary, it was wrong for me to take it out on you and Mary. Forgive me. It is never easy to live as we pray, but I will seek to be kinder the next time I am so exhausted." I kissed them both as I let them out of the car. I drove back to the church, went into my study, and fell on my knees to pray as I never had prayed before. "Lord, you know what a self-centered little boy I still am. After doing your work last night, I was resentful at my exhaustion and unthinkingly hurt my girls. Dear Lord, after preaching to others the love of God that enables us to be at our best even in difficult circumstances, help me not to lose my influence on my own little daughters!"

That prayer did more to break my shell of false demands than any I had prayed in a long time.

I have told the story of the way I came to begin a new discipline of taking the first period each morning in my study to read, think, and verbalize my failures and the way out of them. This was the result of a different kind of crisis through the words of my layman friend who pointed up that with all my good intentions, I had become so busy "building a church" I did not have time to care very much for the people as persons. That really hurt. The words pierced my shell and showed me how inadequate and sick of self-love I really was. I truly *did* care for persons, but I was letting my "must-haves" in regard to building the physical church get in my way. I recall this experience because it points up the fact that without the accepting love of God such a costly self-revelation through the frankness of a friend would have left me in utter despair. I might have left the ministry right then. The one saving element was what the Apostle Paul calls, "the justifying faith" in Christ who, when I accepted his forgiveness and acceptance, gave me the power to accept and forgive myself. Then came the even greater gift of wisdom and courage to begin the disciplines that would let me act more and more in "the maturity of a man in Christ." As Paul puts it so well, "though I have not yet attained, I keep going on to try to possess it for Christ Jesus has already possessed me. Of course, brothers, I really do not think that I have already reached it [maturity in Christ]; the one thing I do, however, is to forget what is behind me and do my best to reach what is ahead. So I run straight toward the goal in order to win the prize" (Phil. 3:12–14, TEV).

Often during these years since I began this honest kind of praying, I have needed to accept my acceptance and to understand my sickness and to start again toward his goal for me. Most of us, if we are truly honest, will need to say many times in effect: Here I stand, one who constantly falls short and knows it, often blinded by prejudice, sick of self-love, capable of hatred and envy, even of fury and violence, one who could have done more for others and for my own better self and did not. I thought I was strong and turned out to be weak, having hurt others and myself. But here I stand, not an outcast or outsider, or counted as a stranger and foreigner, but facing the tremendous fact that I am still a child of God.

What can I do but be glad and accept it all with joy and thanksgiving and then turn to accept and forgive others who are hurting from the betrayal by their false selves and are full of fear, guilt, hostility, and failure. So now I pray, "Father, I accept your forgiveness which I could not possibly deserve even as I accept the grace to forgive others who could not possibly deserve it. I give forgiveness to them. Whether or not they accept it is not my responsibility!" What freedom and creativity are mine with this simple life acceptance!

> What wondrous love is this, O my soul, O my soul,
> What wondrous love is this, O my soul!
> What wondrous love is this that caused the Lord of bliss
> To bear the dreadful curse for my soul, for my soul,
> To bear the dreadful curse for my soul.
>
> —*American Spiritual*

The discipline of thoughtful, prayerful attention to and acceptance of this ever-present giving-love at the heart of the Eternal is the genesis and the fulfillment of life at its best.

Lead us—not into temptation and do not bring us to the test.

The emphasis here is on the first two words *lead us,* rather than on the word *not.* Christian prayer and worship are the acceptance of guidance—the light and leading I need along the perilous way I must go. "*Lead us*—not into temptation."

This is not begging for light and waiting till it comes, but taking one step at a time on faith in the light I have, and the light I see shows the way for another and another and still another step!

As a boy listening to my father, a circuit preacher in New Mexico, I shall not forget one sermon on the text, "The path of the just is a shining light that grows brighter and brighter unto the perfect day." He told the story of a dark night in which his own father took him through a dark path in the woods with only the dim light of a kerosene lantern to show the way. His boyish fright was removed as they went deeper into the darkness. His father talked with him reassuringly and showed him that with each step they took, the lantern lighted the way for the next step.

Obviously this prayer of acceptance of the light for each step is not for the self-willed person who demands his own way. Nor is it for the would-be beginner who has not yet taken the first step and learned to accept the gifts of the Spirit. It is for the committed follower of Christ, whether taking the second or third or three-thousandth step, because he is already surrendered to the higher Will and now *accepts* the insights and leadings necessary. This is not a magical guidance as some religious people claim, making thought and struggle unnecessary, but it is enough light to keep going even in the darkest hour. "My times are in your hands" as the old hymn puts it. "You hold my going that my steps fail not!" cried the psalmist.

I suppose this is the reason for the secularist's greatest skepticism about prayer. Studying history, he reads about many persons, even well-known Christians such as John Calvin, who in the name of Christ burned Servetus at the stake. Servetus, though a good man and a faithful Christian, had differed with Calvin in a crucial part of his theology. Calvin had him burned because he believed that it was Christ's will guiding him to do it! How often this has happened. Many good men and women, believing they were doing right, have prayed for guidance and in the name of Christ have done many foolish, hurtful things. Knowing this, many honest, secular-minded persons have quit praying and abandoned worship.

What they overlook is the world of difference between the one who prays, "Show me your will and I will *then* decide whether or not I want to do it," and the one who prays, "Your will be done, no matter the cost to me—*only show me the way.*" Of course mistakes will be made, but the one least likely to make such mistakes is the person who is utterly willing and open to the truth of highest reality, or who, if he does make mistakes, is the most likely to see them and correct them before too much harm is done!

The acceptance of being lead by a wisdom and love greater than ours is too great a gift to be ignored or denied because of misunderstanding and misuse. Our highest human privilege is to pray with John Henry Cardinal Newman,

> Lead, kindly Light, amid th' encircling gloom,
> Lead thou me on;
> The night is dark, and I am far from home,
> Lead thou me on;
> Keep thou my feet; I do not ask to see
> The distant scene; one step enough for me.

How this leading comes is a mystery, but that it comes is a blessed and irrefutable fact of my own and many other persons' experience.

Looking back over the way I have come, I am sure that my own call to the ministry was one of these experiences. Of course, I cannot prove this, but I believe definitely that my mind was being guided by a Mind greater than my own in the conviction arrived at on Easter Sunday, 1929. I was convinced then as now that the greatest needs of the personal world and my abilities to help meet them all pointed in the direction of the pastoral ministry. No doubt this experience that I call guidance or leading may be partly explained as the result of the example and influence of my parents, of Dr. J. W. Hunt, the president of McMurry College where I was in school, and of others. But the results in my life of a growing dedication to Christ in spite of all my stumbling failures point to the deeper influence of the Spirit then and in the years since. My shell of false self-demands has had to be pierced and crushed many times in costly tests; but in every one of these crushing times, I have made new surrenders of my false self in order to become more of my true self as I am led to believe God intends me to be.

If this is superstition and falsehood, make the most of it! It has certainly produced what to me is life filled with joyous creativity and love. It is to me *truth,* indeed the evidence of life! In submission and acceptance of the loving purposes that God has for me I *have* been *guided* into the positive best ways to meet these "shell-crushing experiences." The most creative periods of my life have followed, without exception, the most costly experiences of failure, or of opposition and injustice.

One "shell-cracking" experience during which I found genuine guidance and help in my disciplines of reading, prayer, and meditation was the result of a real disappointment in my relationships with some of my fellow pastors. Unknown to me there were some misunderstandings of me and my "ambitions," and, as a result, some false and unjust accusations were made by some of my fellow pastors. Hence, I was totally unprepared for the coldness and hostility I felt toward me in a very critical situation in my ministry. The loss to me was not the hardest blow by any means—though naturally I was disappointed. The greatest disappointment was in my brothers' misunderstanding of my motives, the accusations about my position and actions that all who really knew me agreed were unjust and uncalled for.

That night, angry and indignant over the injustice of the accusa-

tions, I had to make a new surrender. I submitted myself again
to Christ and his purposes for me. In the struggle that followed, I
wrote this very honest prayer:
"A terrific day and week . . . Lord, wherein *I* am wrong, *forgive
me*. Wherein I have been wrongfully opposed and accused, *forgive
those who did it*. Grant me, O Holy Spirit of God, the power to
rise above this disappointment and win through to a greater and
stronger love and trust. Help me to love ———— and all of his
followers. They did not really understand what they were doing . . .
Grant me the power to rejoice in your victories and to trust in your
grace. *Amen.*"
   Three days later I was still wrestling with the little demons of
self-will in my subconscious mind. 1 prayed, "O Holy Spirit, enter
the open doors of my heart and teach me all things I need to know
about myself, my motives, my actions. Teach me to serve you . . .
with one simple glad trust. Fill me with peace that all these con-
fusions shall go and I shall be one with you! One in purpose, love,
and power—your greatness infused in my littleness—your wisdom
into my ignorance—your love into my self-centeredness—your mercy
into my needy soul. O Holy Spirit, enter into my heart and teach
me."
   In the following days, I continued to wrestle with the hurts that
had struck deep at my false self-image. Then one morning my
reading brought me precisely to the words I needed. They were
from François de Fénelon. Through his experience and words the
Spirit brought me the very guidance I required: "O man of little
faith!"

> What are you afraid of? Let God act. Abandon yourself to Him.
> You will suffer, but you will suffer with love, peace and consola-
> tion. . . . You will sacrifice your liberty freely and you will enter
> into a new liberty unknown to the world, in which you do nothing
> except for love. . . .
>   The more we love Him, the more we love also all that He makes
> us to do. It is this love that consoles us in our losses, which softens
> our crosses for us, which detaches us from all that is dangerous
> to love, which preserves us from a thousand poisons.[8]

   To be "preserved from a thousand poisons!" I know this was *true*
guidance because this is what began to happen to me. I was preserved

from the poisons of embitterment, jealousy, hatred, and revenge, any one of which would have consumed me. By the end of the month I had won the victory and was able to think and act positively in the year ahead. The guidance led me to see as I wrote in my spiritual notebook, June 29, that I "was placing an importance on something really insignificant compared to my central purpose. Surely," I wrote, "this was needed to deepen my faith, to make me see the mission I was to perform: not to tamper with ecclesiastical machinery in the contest for status—more effectively to preach and teach and heal." And then I wrote this prayer, "O God of hope and love, I praise you who can use this to point my ministry in the right direction. If 'preferment' and honor come, let it be borne with a humility and a love that you can use for your glory and not mine. O Lord, how much it takes of suffering and shock to reveal myself to me. Set me in the right track, O Lord, and keep my spiritual motor running. *Amen."*

And he did just that! I can truthfully say that I grew more in spiritual maturity in the next twelve months than in any other time of my life. This is guidance by the Spirit, for I certainly could not have done it alone. I did forgive and share that forgiveness with the ones who had wronged me. I began to have a new freedom within that led to freedom in my words and actions. I can say truly that this hurt and disappointment were one of the best things that ever happened to me! I know that there is always guidance and deliverance when I am open and ready to see and accept it.

Christian prayer and worship are indeed the *acceptance of deliverance out of temptation and the victory over the evils of our tests. We find guidance and help in the lost and confused, self-directed, frail, and finite way we must go.* As the petition may be freely translated, "Deliver us from the evil—keep us from having to stand the test we are not able to meet."

Of course we are confused. Life is a bewildering chain of events and circumstances that seem to have no rational or meaningful connection. Certainly the events just described seemed totally unrelated to my conception of life as it ought to be. Nevertheless, the choice is yours, as it was mine, to accept the gift of deliverance out of the evil—the ability to stand whatever tests may come—so that we are not utterly overwhelmed. The gift of deliverance is ours even though we cannot see it at the moment and even though the things we do see declare in human feelings that evil, selfishness, hate, pain, and death are really the rulers. But in spite of all I see, visibly, from the human point of view, I affirm and accept the deliverance that is mine.

This experience is in common with disciplined spirits in every age and in every great religion. The true Muslim finds an inner security and peace when he is completely at one with the will of Allah. The devout Hindu is described by Sri Krishna in the *Bhagavad-Gita* as

> That serene one
> Absorbed in the Atman
> Masters his will,
> He knows no disquiet
> In heat or in cold,
> In pain or displeasure,
> In honour, dishonour.
>
> Now that he holds it
> He knows this treasure
> Above all others:
> Faith so certain
> Shall never be shaken
> By heaviest sorrow.[9]

Clearly the disciplines of meditation and commitment to the "Divine Ground within which all partial realities have their being,"[10] has led countless persons to acceptance. This acceptance has been called various names—"resignation," "surrender of the self," "self-renouncement," "self-abnegation." It is this acceptance that has produced what St. François de Sales calls "Holy Indifference" and what the Hindu *Bhagavad-Gita* calls "non-attachment."

> Released from evil
> His mind is constant
> In contemplation:
> The way is easy,
> Brahman has touched him,
> That bliss is boundless.[11]

Since I am dealing with the Christian experience of life in this secular age, I will give several more examples of the undeniable fact in our human experience of those with faith in Christ who have found deliverance in and from the evils that surround us. I point to the fact that such deliverance is held in common only by those who live by a disciplined faith. This experience represents something of what the Apostle Paul would describe as "Christ in you the hope of Glory." The fact that his theological ascription of this deliverance to Christ would not be admitted by Muslim or Hindu or Taoist is not the point. The experiential fact of the deliverance *is* the point. The disciplined Christian who accepts his situation, difficult and costly as it often is, and affirms himself and his relationship with the Eternal Father finds victory. He is "delivered" from the fear and hate and the destruction that follows because he knows that he is in touch with the reality of eternal love which he has seen in Christ. He understands the insistence of Buddha that it is not enough "to know about the ultimate Reality" for to do so is to be compared "to a herdsman of other men's cows." The Christian who knows deliverance in the middle of the evil would appreciate the homelier barnyard metaphor of Mohammed, who said that a philosopher who had not experienced his theorizing about the metaphysical (the nature of reality) "is just an ass bearing a load of books."[12]

While other great religions do bring some genuine guidance and deliverance, or else they would never have continued to have such power over so many persons' thinking and acting, I believe the Christian interpretation of Ultimate Reality is the highest and best. Note I did not say the *only* interpretation. Though I cannot go into a full-length discussion of comparative religions here because of space limitations, let me say that my reasons for making this statement are empirical ones. That is, those who have been most completely committed to Christ as the highest interpretation of Reality have been the ones who over twenty centuries have brought the greatest influences of compassionate and yet wise and strong "giving-love" that dignifies and exalts the person as well as the group or people as a whole. I believe that all the great religions have something to contribute to the establishment of the harmony and peace which would make this the Age of Aquarius, or as Jesus put it, the age in which "the Kingdom of Heaven is here," recognized, accepted, and obeyed. But I believe this quality of self-sacrificing love is most fully represented in Jesus Christ. Without this experience of Christlike love known most effectively to those disciplined in the Christian faith, there is little or no hope that man will find life in this age of megatechnics. Certainly the devotees of all the great religions, instead of fighting each other, should learn from each other and know that the disciplined way of devotion which they share in common must be communicated much more adequately than in the past. For this disciplined way to God is the only hope for the spiritual and moral meanings and unity upon which any true peace and well-being for our human family can depend. Each of us must take the interpretation of that reality that is highest for him and seek to interpret it to others. As Christians we must be tolerant of those who cannot yet see all things summed up in Christ!

One good illustration of this kind of deliverance from evil, even while it threatens our most vulnerable point, is found in the story of Ignatius of Loyola, founder of the Society of Jesus and author of *The Spiritual Exercises.* One day he was asked what he would do if the pope were to decree intolerable restrictions or even an end to his Society of Jesus. He answered immediately, "I would pray about it for fifteen minutes, forget it and go on." His was a detachment—a "holy indifference"—that did not mean a lack of concern but the fullness of a trusting faith and confidence that he was fulfilling a greater purpose than his own and whatever helped this purpose would not fail!

In the same manner every victorious spirit has found deliverance out of the most difficult of experiences that has produced new insights, new hope, new strength. In this sense, prayer and the other spiritual disciplines are therefore not escape or "an opium for the people," as secularists from Karl Marx to the present have called them.

Rufus Jones, the famous Quaker, was for years chairman of the American Friends Service Committee that did so much for the innocent sufferers of World War II as it has in Vietnam and Korea. Yet his whole life was rooted in the discipline of the Spirit, which brought him through some terrifically difficult times such as the death of his only son Lowell and a "nervous breakdown" suffered at the age of fitty. As a result of long periods of overwork, exhaustion, frustration, and no doubt some unresolved emotional problems, this man who "for a whole generation had been the embodiment of optimism, radiant serenity and unbounded energy" found himself at the bottom "in low gear."

"It began to look," he wrote to his daughter, "as if the cloud would never lift." It took a whole year to regain his strength and his old vim. While lying on the beach in Florida, he remembered the figure of speech used by his friend Violet Hodgkin, "Isn't it strange how one has to learn to lie like a star fish on the beach high and dry and cut off from all renewing while the tide rises and falls *just out of reach. . . .* Then at long last . . . the real spring tide comes and floats even one's tired out starfish of a body out into the full flood of life again. Only those who know the deadly weariness of the beach can quite understand the living joy of the ocean when we get back to it once again."[13]

How did he come through to such a deliverance from the depression and low tide which may arrive sooner or later to all? His answer no doubt would be similar to his words at the age of eighty-three as his biographer, Elizabeth Gray Vining, visited with him. He sat in a rocking chair on the porch of his home.

"Yesterday," he said, "I was watching little Willie White playing. He had a wooden duck on wheels which quacked as he pulled it along the driveway. Suddenly something went wrong with the duck; the wheels stopped turning and it stopped quacking. Willie found a soft place on the grass and he lay down on his back and howled. I thought how like the world it was. Something has gone wrong with our duck; it doesn't work anymore, and we lie on the grass and howl."[14]

Rufus Jones had never done that, even at his worst points in life. Instead he had experienced the truth of an editorial he had written after his breakdown:

"Unusual outside weather is only one of our many means of discipline. . . . Much harder is the fight with inside weather and more drearily and pitiless are the fogs and east winds of our human spirits. . . . The fight with stubborn inward weather, the battle with the devil in us, if you will, is the best kind of fighting there is to be done, and he who has conquered the conditions of inner climate has now the best victories that crown men. Not least . . . [is] . . . the further discovery—joyous like that of Columbus sighting a new world—that there are inexhaustible resources of divine grace for those who are resolved to rise above the fog and mist, the sleet and snow of dreary inward weather."[15]

This is surely the wisdom described by Jacques Ellul in the last chapter of his realist book, *Prayer and Modern Man,* which he entitles "Prayer As Combat."[16] Prayer is combat with self. It is combat with the symptoms of our sins such as depression, dejection, and anxiety. It is combat with the false demands of our culture and those around us. It is also combat with God, as we rebel at our circumstances and wrestle as did Jacob at our own river Jabbok until our names are changed and we become "new creations in Christ." This kind of prayer always brings deliverance. It is a million miles from lying in the grass and howling when something is wrong.

Any person who has such a mature faith, ruling not only his conscious mind but increasingly the depths of his unconscious, accepts deliverance even as he accepts food, health, bread. He has a trusting faith. J. P. de Caussade, the great French teacher of Christian Disciplines, called it *Abandonment or Absolute Surrender to Divine Providence.*[17] This abandonment is the acceptance of myself in the living presence of Christ in every event, in history, in my own life, in every moment, even in the darkest hours, believing that my perspective at this time is inadequate to see it all. Indeed I can never see more than a very small part of what is. Mine is a knothole view of life as though I were seeing a baseball game through a knothole in the fence. I may see the batter, but I can't see the pitcher; and when a hit is made, I cannot see for the moment whether it is a fly caught in the outfield or a home run.

I can see only a small part of reality, but God sees it all. "He who is faithful . . . will keep all that I have committed to him against that day" (paraphrase of 2 Tim. 1:12). The alternative is a faith that leads to despair in the end. All the great religions of the world deny this except for the secular religions of humanism, communism, materialism, and scientism! Theirs is a faith in the self-sufficiency of man, somehow believing the modern fairy tale that because man can do everything in the physical world of science he can also conquer his selfishness and greed, his fears and hostility by his own little will. He forgets that he may and generally does *will his own* way which so conflicts with the way of his neighbor that the battle is on. Man has indeed come to a sad end if, knowing that he is finite, held by a thin rope over the abyss of suffering, pain, evil, death, and nothingness, he feels that *no one* has hold of the other end of the rope!

Alice in Wonderland is a child's story, but a remarkably realistic parable of the progress of human life in our earthly wonderland. It also makes clear the need for a guide to help us through the maze of meaninglessness, hatred, and evil, mixed with such beautiful and treasured good.[18]

When Alice walked through the looking-glass and found herself in this bewildering land, everything seemed all mixed up. She was utterly confused as she traveled through a strange country divided into light and dark patches like a chessboard. There were all kinds of odd people—the mad hatter, a friendly rabbit, a mad queen, and a white knight. She could never see how anything made sense. But as the story progresses, we see that each of the events that happened to her "were real moves in a real game." They were ways of taking her from her first experience as a pawn to the eighth square where she would be a queen.

Sometimes the best counsel given seemed most foolish, as when the Rose told her to walk away from the Red Queen if she wanted to meet her! (Compare Jesus' paradox of "losing to find.") It was only when she stopped out of friendliness to help the silly old white Queen by running after her lost shawl, that she jumped over the brook and found herself on the fifth square. And when she thought she was hopelessly lost in the dark forest, with only the crazy advice of the White Knight, she was just emerging to her queenship on the eighth square! But through it all the Hand of the Unseen Player was working to help Alice go from being a pawn to a queen!

Life is certainly not a chess game with God as the player and all of us as pawns. That idea is one of the weaknesses of the Muslim approach to the will of God, as it has been for too many Christians. But our acceptance of the One, who if we let him, "from seeming evil works good for us," will mean that we grow to be kings and queens through all the chances and changes of life. This is the one thing that biographies of the most creative and effective men and women in every age tell us. Some of these are the anonymous men and women who in ordinary ways are accepting the guidance and deliverance that keeps them strong and loving, the salt of the earth and the light of the world!

So when we pray, deliver us from evil, we are not asking that trials and tests which are part of our human lot be reversed. We are asking for deliverance from the evil tendencies of our self-centered egotism. And whether we are young or old in years, we need to be saved from the "old nature" with its cunning disguises and temptations that cause us to fail in the tests. With such continued discipline of trust we accept the step-by-step guidance and the courage not to be swamped by the hurly-burly clash of human wills unsurrendered to anything higher than their own, or by the sudden uprush of our own mad-hatter fears and mad-queen likes and dislikes. We too must walk through the looking-glass of our own egoistic natural consciousness (the false shell) into the blazing day of Reality. This may not come to fruition at once. We may not arrive suddenly at the eighth square where we find ourselves king or queen of our own lives. It may not come in a blaze of sudden light, nor even in this earthly life with all the completeness in store for us. But the symbolic words of the First Epistle of John declare our unwavering faith. "How great is the love that the Father has shown to us! We were called God's children, and such we are; . . . Here and now, dear friends, we are God's children; what we shall be has not yet been disclosed, but we know that when it is disclosed we shall be like him, because we shall see him as he is. Everyone who has this hope before him purifies himself, as Christ is pure" (1 John 3:1-3, NEB).

Yes, there are countless temptations and tests that threaten to pull us aside into the valley of despair and cynical dejection—the "slough of despond" as Christian called his trials in Bunyan's *Pilgrim's Progress*. There are tempting times of hedonistic pleasure that offer illusory promises when we seek to make them central. The pitfalls of such "highs," however arrived at, are the "morning afters," "the withdrawal symptoms," and the hours of depression and self-disgust. But we *can* be delivered from these devils in our unconscious minds as well as from our share of the demons of hate and greed and selfishness that threaten our homes, our cities, our world.

The costly freedom to accept or deny is always ours. Indeed,

> The choice is always ours. Then, let me choose
> The longest art, the hard Promethean way
> Cherishingly to tend and feed and fan

That inward fire, whose small precarious flame,
Kindled or quenched, creates
The noble or the ignoble men we are,
The worlds we live in and the very fates,
Our bright or muddy star.[19]

—*Aldous Huxley*

The best and most productive way to make that choice is in the light of the perspectives and illuminations when, through prayer, meditation, worship, and other spiritual disciplines given to us, we center our attention on Christ. For he is the highest signal we can see of the exalted yet near Reality. The result is the humble, childlike acceptance of the gifts of his bread, forgiveness, guidance, and deliverance as we give ourselves in loving involvement with the lives of our fellow travelers.

Oh, at the point where God and man are one,
Meet me, Thou God; flame on me like the sun;
   I would be part
   Of Thine own heart,
That by my hands Thy love-deeds may be done:
That by my hands Thy love-truths may be shown

. . . .

   That I may bring
   The dead world spring:—
The flowers awake, Lord, at Thy word alone.

   —from "The Immortal and the Mortal,"
   George Barlow[20]

NOTES

1. From a paper presented by Professor Charles Davis at the Consultation on "Worship in a Secular Age" in Geneva, Switzerland, August 1969.

2. Ibid., pp. 1–6.

3. See part 1, pp. 17-19.

4. This is not to indicate that all communes are bad. Their worth depends on the underlying faith and the quality of disciplines that hold them together; that is, the purpose and quality of their leaders.

5. James A. Michener, *The Drifters* (New York: Random House, 1971).

6. Ibid., pp. 691–92.

7. See p. 67.

8. From *Christian Perfection.*

9. *The Song of God: Bhagavad-Gita,* trans. Swami Prabhavananda and Christopher Isherwood (New York: Mentor Books, 1951), pp. 64, 66.

10. Ibid., from the introduction by Aldous Huxley, p. 13.

11. Ibid., p. 67.

12. Ibid., from the introduction, p. 15.

13. E. Vining, *Friend of Life* (Philadelphia: Lippincott, 1958), pp. 150–51.

14. Ibid., pp. 304–5.

15. Ibid., p. 153.

16. Jacques Ellul, *Prayer and Modern Man* (New York: Seabury Press, 1970), pp. 139ff.

17. J. P. de Caussade, *Abandonment or Absolute Surrender to Divine Providence* (New York: Benzinger Brothers, 1887, 1945).

18. See Evelyn Underhill, *Abba* (New York: David McKay, 1960), pp. 73–75.

19. Dorothy Berkley Phillips, ed., *The Choice Is Always Ours* (New York: Richard R. Smith, 1948), frontispiece.

20. *The Oxford Book of English Mystical Verse,* pp. 372–73.

6 The New Song of Caring Love

CELEBRATING THE AGONY AND THE ECSTASY OF
SACRIFICIAL SELF-GIVING

There is one supreme fact of life in the new age which so often
has been overlooked or forgotten by secular man involved so
deeply in megatechnology. Only at the point where God and man
meet and are united in heart and mind may our hands do the
"love-deeds" required. Only where man wills the highest will of the
God of Reality may our minds know the "love-truths" upon which
the life worth living, indeed all human experience, depends.

Prayer and worship and the other spiritual disciplines are the
varied means by which we consciously center our attention and
train our wills to unite our little lives with the great life of the
Father-God. These disciplines are at their highest and best in the
joyous celebration of the victory won by the Christ of caring-love
on the cross. The victory, however, did not end with Jesus' cross.
It has been and is now present in the lives of thousands who have
caught the spirit of the Son of man and Son of God bearing the
cross for others. But it is a celebration that includes more than the
emotions stirred or the mind enlarged. It is a celebration that leads
to the life involved in sacrificial self-giving love with our fellows
in the family of God.

The truth is simple: we cannot separate the agony from the
ecstasy. That too often Christians and other religious persons have
tried to do so is the best commentary on the emptiness and failures
of much we call worship.

Among those who are seeking a renewal of vital prayer and
worship today there is a great deal of emphasis on celebration. But

148

the mere fact that the liturgy of personal prayer and public worship may now include new forms calling for joyous celebration is no guarantee that we will really worship. The use of these new forms will not in themselves unite our minds and our wills with the Eternal Spirit "whose name is Love, whose nature is compassion, in whose will is our perfect freedom and in the knowledge of whom stands our eternal life."[1]

Celebration is a very great part of Christian worship, depending altogether on what and how we celebrate! We have had a rash of what is called "contemporary worship." Most of it has been sincerely planned to make worship real to secular persons, especially youth who have been turned off by the use of "the same old thing," the meaning and value of which they never understood in the first place. Some of this contemporary worship has been very helpful. Much of it has been a failure because, like other worship in the past, it has been *contrived* and those coming to meet God have been *manipulated* into feelings and acts that were not honest or intelligent.

Certainly Christian worship must be *enthusiastic* and *joyful,* if it is indeed to be the celebration of the mighty realities of God's caring love in the Christ of yesterday, today, and forever. There are so many good things and pleasures given for us to enjoy, we ought to celebrate them with thankfulness and praise. The lack of this joyous, wholehearted enthusiasm when the Good News of life abundant is proclaimed and celebrated in word, act, and song is what makes worship boring, dull, and dead for so many.

If you find worship dull, either as a public or private experience, it is for two simple reasons: (1) for you there is no sense of the immediacy of the presence of God, and, therefore, (2) nothing really happens even though you are physically present at what is called worship and even though you are pumping up what you hope to be effective prayer.

Christian worship at its best is keen awareness of and response to the living God who in Christ is present and acting in human life and in all the universe. From the very beginning Christian worship has been characterized as joyous, meaningful celebration, something to look forward to rather than to avoid. The disciples were taught to worship as Jesus did, by his word and example. They worshiped together not only on the mountain and in homes but with him went every Sabbath "as was his custom" to the synagogue.

Imagine the electrifying experience in the synagogue in Nazareth that day as Jesus stood up to read from the Prophet Isaiah.

The spirit of the Lord is upon me because he has anointed me;
He has sent me to announce good news to the poor,
To proclaim release for prisoners and recovery of sight for the blind;
To let the broken victims go free,
To proclaim the year of the Lord's favour.
Today . . . in your very hearing this text has come true.

(Luke 4:18–19, 21, NEB)

"The Kingdom of God is here . . . has come very near to you." Their celebration of this proclamation was so joyous that the Pharisees asked Jesus why his disciples did not fast and worship with sad solemnity as did the disciples of John the Baptist. His answer was plain, "Can you make the bridegroom's friends fast while the bridegroom is with them?" (Luke 5:34, NEB). In their encounter with him, they had met the Son of the Father and had seen evidences of the glorious Kingdom of God (Heavenly Reality) in which life is full and satisfying and crowned with joyful love and peace.

Even on the last night together with its sad and tragic overtones for their finite minds, there was a celebration. "The Lord Jesus on the night when he was betrayed took bread, and when he had given thanks, he broke it, and said, 'This is my body which is for you. Do this in remembrance of me.' In the same way also the cup, after supper, saying, 'This cup is the new covenant in my blood. Do this, as often as you drink it, in remembrance of me' " (1 Cor. 11:23–25, RSV).

The breaking and giving of bread and the sharing of the cup in memory of him became the joyful occasion of highest worship called the Eucharist, the giving of thanks. For though Jesus was going through the agony of facing the cross, he led them that night to a joyful note of hope and victory. "And when they had sung a hymn, they went out to the Mount of Olives" (Matt. 26:30, RSV). We do not know exactly which of the psalms they sang. We may be sure it was one that celebrated with thanksgiving God's victory in creation and in the redemption which he was about to show forth in the coming events!

True, it was a celebration on *faith*, for in Gethsemane as he was left alone while his disciples slept, he prayed in great agony, "My Father, if it be possible, let this cup pass from me; nevertheless, not as I will, but as thou wilt" (Matt. 26:39, RSV). And as he hung in the excruciating pain and suffering of the cross, he felt as we do, forsaken and alone, and he cried, "My God, my God, why hast thou forsaken me?" (Matt. 27:46, RSV). But the remembrance of the disciples declares that he also prayed in utter commitment, "Father, into thy hands I commit my spirit!" (Luke 23:46, RSV). The disciples' memory of those dark hours contains a strange but wonderful note of joy. Though his prayer and worship were completely realistic in recognizing the evil, the suffering, and the pain of our common life which he bore, there was also joy. As the author of Hebrews pictures it, "Jesus, . . . who for the joy that was set before him endured the cross, despising the shame" (Heb. 12:2, RSV).

This note of ecstasy in the agony—the joy even on the cross—is the most amazing and wonderful fact of our Lord's human experience, as it may be our own. The words of Jesus in the last hour in the upper room are unforgettable. "I have spoken thus to you, so that my joy may be in you, and your joy complete" (John 15:11, NEB). "Peace is my parting gift to you, my own peace, such as the world cannot give. Set your troubled hearts at rest, and banish your fears" (John 14:27, NEB). "But courage! The victory is mine: I have conquered the world" (John 16:33, NEB).

No doubt these words and attitudes of Jesus seemed strangely out of place during the dark hours of the crucifixion and the entombment. They were remembered with fresh meaning as the experiences of his resurrection were known. At Pentecost the disciples at last began to understand with a tremendous leap of faith that their friend Jesus was alive in the Holy Spirit—the risen Christ who is the Lord of all creation (see Eph. 1 and 2).

Since Jesus Christ is Lord, there is no agony of human evil and pain too great to be met with the ecstasy of faith and hope. No wonder the note of joy rings throughout the New Testament and in all authentic Christian experience. No wonder that early Christian worship was always a happy occasion. Whether in the "church in their house" or in the catacombs underneath the city of Rome where they met to escape the bloody persecution of a succession of Roman emperors from Nero to Diocletian, their worship was filled with a boundless and overflowing exaltation and delight! Here they celebrated the Eucharist—at daybreak as one of the Roman writers portrayed, "these Christians meet to sing a hymn to Christ as God." This glorious note of celebration is reflected in the Book of Revelation. This book contains the only description of worship found in the New Testament. Scholars believe it describes not only the worship in the future at the consummation of God's victory in Christ, but also the way in which the early church celebrated the victory that had already been won in Christ. This celebration was triumphant. Though none could see with physical vision its final consummation, they knew the victory was already there! "But thanks be to God, which giveth us the victory through our Lord Jesus Christ" (1 Cor. 15:57, KJV). "Delight yourselves in God; yes, find your joy in him at all times" (Phil. 4:4, Phillips).

This experience of joyous victory, "the realized eschaton," is but a promise of the victory that is to come. "The Kingdom of God is near" had been Jesus' recurring theme. The Kingdom of Heavenly Reality is the way things are. The deepest and highest truth of our universe is the rule of Christ at God's right hand—the symbolic way of saying that the Spirit controlling the power behind and through the universe is Christ the Lord! Believing this, Christians have celebrated in words, music, and ritual acts the victory which is now theirs and will be revealed in its fullness in God's good time. For there is "nothing in all creation that can separate us from the love of God in Christ Jesus our Lord" (Rom. 8:39, NEB).

With this in mind read John's description of the worship of the early church. As you read seek to translate these ancient symbols into meanings that are as real today as then. "Then I looked, and I heard around the throne and the living creatures and the elders the voice of many angels, numbering myriads of myriads and thousands of thousands, saying with a loud voice, 'Worthy is the Lamb who was slain, to receive power and wealth and wisdom and might and honor and glory and blessing!' And I heard every creature in heaven and on earth and under the earth and in the sea, and all therein, saying, 'To him who sits upon the throne and to the Lamb be blessing and honor and glory and might for ever and ever!' And the four living creatures said, 'Amen!' and the elders fell down and worshiped" (Rev. 5:11–14, RSV).

What does this really mean, beyond the translation of ancient symbols into modern meanings? How do we celebrate the victory

—the agony with the ecstasy—in the middle of our confused and chaotic lives? This is the crux of the question of vital prayer and worship.

There is no simple answer, but in the last chapter, I would add as much as I am able from my own experience and my interpretation of the experience of others to an understanding of the disciplines of conscious thought and attention in the use of words, of music, of ritual acts, and of shared silence and study. By these means our prayer and worship may indeed be true celebrations that exalt our vision and bring illumination and power to our minds and acts. Thus we live in the real world of technology and of vital personal relationships with the unseen as well as the seen—but only as our spiritual disciplines lead us by the love of God to the ecstasy that is never far from the agony of costly, caring love.

THE CELEBRATION MUST BE AUTHENTIC

Clearly I am in favor of a recovery of the genuine enthusiasm that accompanies true worship. Nevertheless I must warn all who read this as I warn myself (especially those who plan corporate worship for others and who study for more effective personal prayer lives) that the enthusiasm and joy of the true celebration of our Gospel-Reality cannot be pumped up or contrived. Nor can those who worship be manipulated into the celebration of the victory of life in the presence of Christ. This is as true of many in modern "contemporary" worship, as it was in the days when "revival techniques" were often used for the same purpose. For if we attempt to manipulate and force a contrived celebration it will be, and often is, just that—contrived, artificial, superficial. If after the songs and shouts and emotional release are over, there is a let-down, and life goes on in the same old indifferent, self-centered way, we are worse off than if we had not tried to worship! We may arrive at the deadly sin of dejection, like the man who is apathetic about apathy! And who doesn't give a ———.

This is often the tragic experience of so many youth who by the thousands attend the rock festivals. Here many of the characteristics of human worship in general are found. We must remember that of course there are other kinds of worship such as the celebrations of nationalism, communism, fascism, sex orgies, and the like. We may celebrate by eating and drinking together, by singing, through physical action, and through the actualization of community. "It is wonderful to feel we belong." It is good to enjoy spontaneity and freedom to be oneself, to act naturally. Most of these are valuable. Obviously the lack of some of these is often what helps make much that is called Christian worship dull, boring, dead.

Some of these can become helpful aids to worship. Their value, however, depends on the spirit and meaning behind their use. Their lack is indicated by the fact that they are not the chief disciplines of mind and will that lead to the perspectives, illumination, acceptance, and life dedication in loving self-sacrifice so desperately needed today. This is what Charles Davis was saying at the World Consultation on Worship.

> Updated Christian thought is no more acceptable to the truly secular man than the ancient variety; indeed rather less so, because the secular man often retains a respect for the consistency of the traditional. I think this same applies to updated Christian worship. Despite the guitars and folk singing, despite the colloquial language and comradely informality contemporary forms of Christian worship remain essentially at variance with secular consciousness.[2]

He hastened to point out that he was not minimizing the values of more meaningful language and forms, or the use of guitars and folk singing. Neither was he saying that the emphasis on preservation of the traditional is the answer.

> Christian worship is not the savouring of historic ritual (or updated contemporary ritual) but the expression of Christian faith in forms that will engage the whole man.[3]

Indeed Christian worship may and should include many helpful new forms and more understandable words. Its genuine test, however, is whether or not it is the door to life in the Kingdom of God—the rule of Reality as seen in Jesus' life and spirit and supremely in his sacrificial love that met the test on the cross of suffering and shame. And this kind of self-giving love is not a part of the secular man's background and training!

Zona Gale illustrates the difficulty with secular man in her parable of the two tadpoles in the pond. One stuck his head out of the water for a moment and returned to say to the other tadpole, "There is a vast, terrible and wonderful world out there, and it could obliterate us if it wanted to." But the second tadpole answered, "You are a fool, besides that kind of talk is other worldliness!"

So let us be honest. When in our meditation, reading, prayer, and worship we talk about "celebrating the victory of Christ," the secular within us cries, "What victory?" From the tadpole view of the secular world consciousness, Jesus was only a good man, a little foolish perhaps, who got in trouble with his own people and with the Romans who joined in putting him to death on the cross. He left a few wise teachings that are mostly too idealistic to take seriously. But where is any victory in a world which can go up in an atomic explosion and where with all our science we still despise, hate, and kill each other?

This means that as human tadpoles talking about the victory of the love of Christ we are talking other-wordly nonsense which is impractical, foolish, and distracting. We know we had better find some way to love and work together, but if we do, we feel it will be through Arthur Koestler's psychopharmacological pill, or the psychologists' and psychiatrists' adjustment, or the sociologists' planning. This is the reason why it is difficult for most of us to "delight ourselves in the Lord, to find our joy in him at all times."

So we go back to the premises of the first chapter: faith that is living and vital is becoming convinced, reconciled, committed, and then disciplined in a new consciousness, which Paul described a long time ago. "From now on, therefore, we regard no one from a [purely] human point of view; even though we once regarded Christ from a human point of view, we regard him thus no longer. Therefore, if any one is in Christ, he is a new creation; the old has passed away, behold, the new has come" (2 Cor. 5:16–17, RSV). This means that "worship is the act of standing outside of our normal consciousness in order to become aware of God and to respond to him."[4] Worship that brings "the new creation" able to love self-sacrificially with great joy requires a "world-transcendence."

Only through a belief in the existence of the supernatural—that is, a reality that transcends the reality of the natural world of everyday life—can man grasp the true proportions of his experience.[5]

That is, we have to rise above a tadpole view of our little pond. For we must do more than stand *inside* our normal consciousness and see things in the way they appear to the world that recognizes nothing which cannot be measured and tested by physical or psychological sciences. If this is the way we see life, the question of joyous celebration in the time of sorrow and the necessity to bear a cross for others is just plain silly.[6]

Worship and prayer, as Christians have found them real in everyday life, are the acts by which we stand *outside* our "normal human consciousness," or what we call "normal," to see the world that really is. Indeed this is the truly *normal* consciousness because it is directed toward the deepest and highest realities that have sent up all kinds of "signals of transcendence" for those who are open to see them and to act by faith on them—the witness of the words and lives of the most victorious spirits of all ages.

The test of any authentic spiritual discipline, including the most emotion-filled celebration, is whether or not it opens the door for us and through us for others to the Kingdom of caring love, where the agony and the ecstasy are united, and where we join our lives with the creative, redemptive action of God on earth with other persons. "Without the shedding of blood there is no forgiveness of sins" (Heb. 9:22, RSV) is a phrase that when misunderstood repels many. But when it is seen in the light of the blood of human life poured out for others, it should be taken very seriously today—this day when the blood of so many innocent as well as guilty is being shed unnecessarily!

NO JOYOUS SONG WITHOUT GENUINE SACRIFICE

As a young pastor, I was shocked to hear a great preacher, Dr. George Arthur Buttrick, say that if we really understood the prayer of our Lord with its demands for trust and commitment and costly personal involvement with God and his family in all their evil and sufferings, many, if not most, of us would hesitate or even refuse to pray it. As it is, too often when we use this great prayer taught us by our Lord, we rattle it off so fast that it is without meaning, as are many other of our "acts of worship." When this happens, our worship is useless and even harmful.

The ancient Hebrew prophet, Amos, was declaring this immutable truth when he cried to the nominal worshipers of his day, "These are the words of the Lord the God of Hosts:

> I hate, I spurn your pilgrim-feasts;
> I will not delight in your sacred ceremonies.
> When you present your sacrifices and offerings
> I will not accept them, . . .
> Spare me the sound of your songs;
> I cannot endure the music of your lutes.
> Let justice roll on like a river
> and righteousness like an ever-flowing stream."
> (Amos 5:21–24, NEB)

Indeed it is costly and dangerous to pray, "Your kingdom come, your will be done on earth, in our common life, as it is in the Heaven of Reality," for his will includes justice for all and a rightness that goes beyond the forms of piety that make us feel safe and secure without calling us to work for justice and righteousness! It is costly to pray, "Forgive us as we forgive, give us our daily bread as we have helped others to get their daily bread. Deliver us from the evil, even as we help to deliver others from evil."

There is another side to the picture. The more we really pray this prayer the better able we are to accept the perspective of the present rule of God in Christ with his priceless gifts of bread, forgiveness, guidance, and deliverance for ourselves. Then we will understand that this kind of prayer is the single most important action of any human life and we will be increasingly eager to pray it.

The difficulty is that the last half of this great prayer is as often misunderstood as the first half—the obvious reason so many of us use the words glibly without really praying and acting on our prayers! For we all want bread, both physical and spiritual. We all want to be loved, accepted, and forgiven. We want to be led out of temptation that would really hurt and to be delivered from the evil that could destroy us. And we want these also for our loved ones and in a general sort of way for others.

The mighty truth of the rule of God in human life is simple but immutable: none of these precious gifts are ours unless we are ready and willing to be involved lovingly and caringly with others in sharing these gifts. Surely this is the clear meaning of Jesus' parable of the final judgment (Matt. 25:42–45, NEB). In various other teachings Jesus made clear that our receiving forgiveness and mercy are dependent on our giving forgiveness and mercy.

Unless you care about another's bread you will be hungry.

The only way you can find forgiveness is to forgive.

The only way to be delivered from evil is as you share with me in delivering others. "For whoever would save his life will lose it; and whoever loses his life for my sake, he will save it" (Luke 9:24, RSV).

That is, if we are to find and share life in the Age of Aquarius, we are required by the very nature of our lives in their deepest relationships to recognize and accept the disciplines of Christian prayer and worship. They will become for us a life - consciously lived in the perspective of faith in and communion with God our Father with whom we are involved in the same loving, redemptive, reconciling task as he is. That is to say, since God the Ultimate Reality was in Christ reconciling, hugging the world to himself, we cannot be anything less than reconcilers, bridging the gap between ourselves and God as we bridge the gap between ourselves and others. Only then will we pray with our lives, as well as with our words, such a prayer as that of St. Francis, "Lord, make me an instrument of Thy peace!" Dag Hammarskjöld realized this better than most moderns when in his spiritual diary *Markings* he indicated that his own "faith in God demands realization in action: 'In our era the road to holiness (wholeness, maturity) necessarily passes through action.' "[7] But as Gustaf Aulén, his best interpreter, points out, "this strong accent on action he combines with a similar emphasis on stillness and silence, terms familiar to the mystics. Such quietness does not call only for a pause in a life overspent with work; it calls for constant, restful communion with God in order to find strength."[8] This is not only the *ideal* for humanity, it is the *real*—the only way life will work, either personally, or in the family, or in the society of peoples and nations. Whenever we refuse to recognize and pray this prayer and live as we pray, we are going against the grain—we are in hell. As Thomas Merton puts it so vividly,

> Hell is where no one has anything in common with anybody else except the fact that they all hate one another and cannot get away from one another and from themselves.

They are all thrown together in their fire and each one tries to
thrust the others away from him with a huge, impotent hatred.
And the reason why they want to be free of one another is not so
much that they hate what they see in others, as that they know
others hate what they see in them: and all recognize in one another what they detest in themselves, selfishness and impotence
and agony and terror and despair.

The tree is known by its fruits. If you want to understand the
social and political history of modern nations, study hell.[9]

Hence if one would enter and help his fellows, his home, his
country, his world live in the Kingdom of Heavenly Reality, the
first requirement is this commitment in thought and prayer that
leads to action by which the caring love of Christ is reproduced in
us and through us to our world!

One of the most disturbing yet illuminating stories I have read
making this truth clear is told in the unusual yet human account of
an Episcopal priest, James Holroyd, who found himself pushed into
the Christian ministry without adequate motivation and discipline.[10]
He enrolled in the seminary and continued through his ordination
and first years of service as a parish priest through a series of experiences in which he was continually being hurt by and hurting
others. He had grown up in a home with his grandmother and aunt
giving him stringent puritanical controls with only a semblance of
genuine love. Lacking such love during the major part of his life, he
was incapable of loving in the responsible Christian sense. Because
of this lack of loving acceptance and of his own ego drives, he permitted others to use him in their own destructive passion for pleasure and power. His roommate in college, Nord Carlson, seemed
always to be secure with plenty of money, but turned out to be a
thief and a homosexual. Holroyd protected Nord from the police
and then abandoned him in his moment of greatest loneliness and
need, because as usual he did not care enough to get involved in
helping him. One night after walking out on Nord, Holroyd returned to find the boy dead, hanging by several of Holroyd's ties
in the closet of their bedroom.

James Holroyd entered the seminary and was ordained to the
priesthood without very much if any Christlike concern to serve.
His motivation was rather a sense of guilt and a succession of events
that made it easier for him to take this route than any other. His

old pastor, without examining the youth's motives or fitness for the ministry, gave him the first push because, as Holroyd later described, he was more interested in getting another "merit badge for shoving me into the seminary!"

The bishop to whom the youth was sent to talk about studying for the priesthood was the uncle of Nord Carlson, his former roommate who had hanged himself. The bishop soon discovered that the young man before him had been his nephew's roommate. When Holroyd confessed, "I was his last chance for life, and I told him to go to hell the night he died," the ecclesiastic grimly tightened the noose of the professional ministry around the young man's neck, saying, "I see, and you are here to take his place."

With such inadequate motivation, it was to be expected that James Holroyd would not find reality in the expressions of his faith or in his ministry of counseling, administration, and the leadership of worship. Indeed the story of his years in the seminary and the first period of his service as a priest contain an unbelievable series of inept, selfish, and destructive relationships. That is, they are unbelievable for anyone who has not known others who have foolishly tried to be "professional Christians" without genuine faith and intelligent life disciplines. His life and ministry, though well intentioned much of the time, continually caused hurt and tragedy rather than healing and hope. Obviously he was "living out of the shell" of false goals and drives, most of which he did not recognize.

One day he attended a lecture by a well-known psychologist whose books and articles he had read and of whom he had a high opinion. Late the second night of the seminar the psychologist was talking about how dangerous the pastoral ministry is for lay people "who with a desperate but misplaced trust put themselves in the hands of a pastor who has a serious and unsolved problem of his own that he is avoiding." He was describing the kind of Christians so many of us are. Our outer "shells" of ego demands are so thick that our true selves rarely if ever get an opportunity to be seen much less fulfilled. In such a relationship with ourselves, with God, and with others, whether we are ordained ministers or laymen, there is always more hurt and confusion than health and clarity. The psychologist went on to describe the fact that some pastors damaged and sometimes contributed to the destruction of as many persons as they helped and saved to new life.

Holroyd could no longer escape facing his own ineptitude and failure as a person and as a priest. He began to see the faces of those whose lives he had harmed by his own lust and self-centered demands. Some of these were among those to whom he had attempted to minister as pastor. He realized that he had helped curse them even as he had fed them on the thin pablum of a superficial religion.

"A great wave of hopelessness, a sense of tragedy and guilt, swept over me," he wrote later describing that eventful night. "I had never experienced such anxiety, panic and depression, all at the same time. Now I began to understand the true meaning of the word *angst* [anxiety]. It was more than dread. It was the end of everything."

He ran out of the room into the streets, unconscious of the cold rain that drenched him. He went to his room, but there he felt himself "trapped by the forces of evil which I had cockily unleashed against myself. I had underestimated reality again." He abandoned his room and ran out into the night rain again. Staggering wildly, he fell over a fence and then a garbage pail. With utter self-disgust, he lifted the lid and tried to hide in the garbage. Sickened by the smell, he flung himself on the ground, hugging the garbage pail and wretching. Then he rose and staggered on for another hour until he came to a little white church lighted dimly within. Covered with the stench from the garbage and his own sickness, he crawled down the aisle and flung himself on the floor in front of the altar. Here he slept for a few hours. When he awoke, a black man was standing over him. This black man, the priest of the little church, reached out and touched him *lovingly*. Somehow the priest understood that "I was not sleeping off cheap wine or spirits but had been the playground of another kind of spirit." The priest still did not speak but went out to return with a cup of coffee for each. As they drank the coffee, the understanding pastor "gradually drew from me the terrors of the night, the ghostly foe, the spots of sin, and the whole phantasmagoria." Then he "made the sign of the cross on my forehead, gave me absolution and his blessing."

"As he struggled to his feet . . . he said, 'My brother.' (*My brother!?*) 'Mass is at seven. Do you feel well enough to serve me?' "

Holroyd managed to get through the service, hearing only "snatches of the Holy Mysteries. *'He saves your life from destruction*

*. . . He crowns you with mercy . . . with well-doing put to silence
the ignorance of foolish men . . . not using your liberty as a cloak
for malice . . . your heart shall rejoice.'* "[11]

This was a celebration of true worship—the agony with the
ecstasy—in which James Holroyd began to face himself and to
come alive to the person he could be. He wrote, "At least I came
to grips with the problem of the possible validity of my vocation
to the priesthood." He cultivated the habit of spending an hour
every evening sitting quietly in the chapel. "I did not have any cozy
talks with the Lord. I did not grind out the Daily Office of Evening
Prayer, nor did I immerse myself in [false] pietism or drench my
soul in prayers strung out like washing on a line. . . . I sat evening
after evening chewing the cud of the Gospel."

The result of placing himself "in this kind of spiritual climate"
was to "uncrease my mind." He began to understand that the reasons
propelling him into the ministry were not adequate. He discovered
that "he had to have different and better reasons" for continuing as
a Christian and as a minister. Then he describes what is true for
every one of us who would celebrate the joy even in the pain. "I
have learned that it is warfare all the time . . . that I cannot desert
my vocation any more than I can out run my shadow. . . . When
I fall I get up again. . . . There is only one way to regard the
stupefying spectacle of life, and that is if it didn't make sense, then
God would have never have taken it on. I owe him a death anyway."[12]

Indeed James Holroyd began to find life through this death to
himself and his false images. The next ten years including several
after his election as Bishop of Huntington were filled with peace
and joy and caring love.

He received this new life first through the black pastor who called
him "Brother" and touched him "lovingly." It was given to him by
the power of accepting Father-God through the acts and words of
the Eucharist. He also found it through the self-sacrificing love
of Diana, the first woman he had met who would not let him "use"
her, but who taught him the glory of mutual self-giving in love that
is so much more than sexual gratification. They were married and
their life together was filled with harmony and a deep happiness
he had not previously known. James Holroyd's story ends in a
double murder, the result of one of his past revengeful acts. This
book is primarily a sordid story of human folly and sin, but its

conclusion declares the truth of the words Holroyd read in that first true worship which he conducted with the black brother minister in the little white church.

> He saves your life from destruction. . . . He crowns you with mercy . . . not using your liberty as a cloak for malice . . . *your heart shall rejoice!*

The agony with the ecstasy—but the ecstasy conquers the agony! To be thus involved and equipped for our life and ministry, whether ordained or lay, is indeed the apex and result of Christian prayer at its best. As I have pointed out in several other places, this is not prayer and worship as magical, superstitious hocus pocus, presumptive attempts to use God for our own exaltation or peace and personal or group security. It is no escape from life—no opiate. Rather it is the opposite: an open-eyed acceptance of life at its best in loving cooperation and fellowship with my brothers and sisters in God's great family. Without this, our prayer and worship are indeed delusions and a curse on us and our fellows.

Caring Involvement: The Summit of Christian Prayer and Worship As Its Conclusion and Result

In this sense, therefore, it is impossible to say where prayer and worship end and work and service begin. Certainly when Jesus put his hands on the eyes of the blind and on the limbs of the lame and leprous, when he held little children in his arms and when out of love for the loveless and lost of his day and every day he bore his cross to Calvary, he was praying just as when he was alone at the mountain top.

How strange that we set the one action apart from the other in our lives or in his. Indeed he needed withdrawal to the *solitude* of the desert and mountain without which his return to the valley of *action* and service would have been impossible or at least ineffective. If the withdrawal was necessary for him, it surely is for us! At the very beginning, he spent forty days and nights, and many other times he withdrew for a whole night in prayer and rest. But remember, his prayer life continued as he came down the mountain and walked out on the common roads of Galilee and at last to the cross.

Hence, those who prepare the bulletin for the worship of the gathered congregation must be careful not to put at the bottom of the order of worship, "Worship ends; service begins." For worship is a service to God and man, and service is worship carried to its highest level. Both are required, and he who would do one without the other is running against the cutting edge of the sharp sword of divine-human truth by which life is either enriched and made noble or hurt and destroyed.

Obviously separation of work and worship, prayer and life, is one of the main reasons some people have abandoned prayer and worship as "worn out" and "irrelevant." It is a sad fact that for many their kind of prayer and worship has too often been a private piety of escape, a quest for private peace of mind, a culture religion that is a delusion and a curse.

The other side of the story, however, is also true. To be fed, forgiven, led, and delivered from evil by the Lord through the ministry of the gathered community of believers in worship and fellowship and through the personal disciplines of prayer and meditation do give us a priceless peace of mind. Here is the only way to "the peace of God that passes understanding." This is the pathway to courage even in the face of opposition and death. This kind of spiritual discipline does make a nation and a people great and fruitful. But when worship is used primarily for individual or national escape from the demand of caring for others or for false comfort that "is not concerned with the afflictions of Joseph," it is indeed a curse rather than a blessing. That kind of false piety must and will go!

So if we abandon this false piety, as we must, there is still required a vital piety to take its place—a discipline of prayer, study, worship, and fellowship to supply insight into God's will and daily strength and courage to fulfill it. We must have the discipline to accept the deliverance required from the treacherous enemy of our own self-willed pride with its ugly children of self-pity, envy, prejudice, and hate, and we must also accept the victory over those fears and hostilities that result. Such a piety, call it what you will, is the most important of all human disciplines.

One more true story is appropriate here to illustrate the necessity for the kind of spiritual disciplines which seek to let the Spirit of eternal Love *use* us rather than the other way round. So often we are like the very self-sufficient, successful sales manager of a large company who had some costly experiences before he learned the difference in the two kinds of piety. He had come to worship occasionally as a member of the church of which I was pastor. When he shook hands with me, it was with the condescending spirit of a wealthy patron who congratulated God and me that he had taken the time from his busy life to attend church. He really did not think he needed worship much less a discipline of prayer, reading, and meditation. His life had no room for these things which he would leave for weaker men.

At least so he told me when I first really got to know him. It was on the ninth floor, the psychiatric section, of a large hospital. He had hit the bottom, at last. He had crossed over the line from a compulsive drinker to become an alcoholic. His business relationships were almost ruined. His health was wrecked. His home was on the rocks. His wife and children were through with him. His last shred of self-confidence was gone as he looked up at me with the humble appeal, "Can you help me?"

I answered as honestly as I knew how that it all depended on his openness and willingness to learn not just from me but from the Spirit who was seeking to teach him and lead him through all the suffering he had imposed on himself and others by trying to play God. I explained what this meant, and he responded with great openness to my confession that I had suffered from the same sin he had, only my symptoms were different. I said I had not become an alcoholic—"maybe I would have if I had used it. Perhaps I am a dry alcoholic. But I have other symptoms just as hurtful." I shared with him some of my struggles with envy and jealousy, with hostility toward those who got in my way. Having established a beachhead where both of us were on the same level with much in common, I proceeded to help him draw his own self-picture. We used the chart (see page 107) with the heart and the shell to help make clear that his alcoholism was only a symptom. He had to find the cause. Over a period of weeks I saw him an hour every two or three days and led him to an understanding of the prayer that brings acceptance, perspective, illumination, and the ability to love. He made the first timid experiment and then wholeheartedly began to pray and then to get well. At the same time I was teaching his wife and two adolescent children something of the same truth and helping them to a reconciliation. (Such an opportunity, by the way, is the finest privilege any person can have in this life.) It was great indeed to see him and his family reconciled and grow together.

Then he was out of the hospital, taken back to his former job, and with his family sitting out in front of me every Sunday. That is, for awhile. Then I missed him. One day I was called back to the hospital and found him flat on his back again.

"What's the matter with me, Lance?" he asked piteously. "I thought I was doing everything you taught me. What went wrong?"

"Well," I asked, "did you continue your prayers? I noticed you have ceased your regular worship."

He apologized for the latter. "I just became too busy, but I didn't stop saying my prayers."

"What were you praying? What did you want in your prayers?"

"I asked God to keep me sober and to help me keep my home and my job," he answered.

"That is, you *used* prayer as a means of *manipulating* God and his powers to help you keep your old image of yourself and your life and home just as it was. Could that be the reason?"

"I hadn't thought of that." (I realized how little he had understood my previous teaching.) "Do you mean that I was trying to *use* God, instead of asking him to use *me?*"

"What do you think?" I countered. "Is this not what Jesus meant when he said, 'Our Father, *your* Kingdom come, *your* will be done'?"

He suddenly realized the simple but tragic reason for his failure. In the weeks that followed he sought to offer up his life where God needed him most. He and his wife became vital, active members of a serving church. He began to find ways to serve those about him. He and his wife are articulate and self-sacrificing followers of the one who came not to be ministered unto but to minister. The difference was a true piety of prayer, worship, and loving action rather than a false piety of pagan magic, seeking to use God to get and keep a self-exaltation of status and comfort! What a difference!

WHO WILL BE WILLING AND ABLE TO PAY THE COST OF CARING?

The answer to this question is the key to the two major problems that confront us as we seek to live an authentic Christian discipleship—a life of ministry, ordained or lay, of caring involvement in the deepest needs and hurts of others. For who really wants to get involved in so costly a way and who really wants to discipline himself?

The answer is, *no one,* unless we have glimpsed at least the beginning of the true perspective of Christian prayer which can enable us to be aware of who we are and what are the promises and resources for us and our fellows in the light of God's loving reality in Christ. Unless we accept the gifts of illumination, courage, and the deep peace of soul that can face the worst having met and conquered our fears, we will avoid getting involved. For "courage is fear that has said its prayers," and certainly we need such courage. Let's face it. None of us wants to get involved in such a costly ministry, and we will not do so unless we have heard God's trumpets of new creation every morning!

An old Jewish legend has it that when Satan was asked after falling from heaven what it was he missed most, he answered, "I think what I miss most is the sound of trumpets every morning." God's trumpets every morning are sounding, but only he who is awake to listen and to obey will find the marching orders and the daily rations and the presence of our Captain to lead us on in costly but glorious self-giving! We can take the agony with the joy only in the ecstasy of daily renewed faith! As Evelyn Underhill, the great British teacher of Christian disciplines, declares:

> If the transforming power of religion is to be felt, its discipline must be accepted, its price paid in every department of life; and it is only when the soul is awakened to the reality and call of God, known at every point of its multiple experience, that it is willing to pay the price and accept the discipline. Worship is a primary means of this awakening.
>
> It follows once more that whole-hearted adoration is the only real preparation for right action: action which develops within the Divine atmosphere, and is in harmony with the eternal purposes of God.[13]

So we might ask, why care for others in their troubles, sufferings, and sins? We might do it in a nice sheltered place in some peaceful valley separated from the roar of human hatred and hell. But this isn't the kind of world we live in. Our world has violence in hearts, homes, streets, and suicidal wars between races and peoples. There is untold suffering in Southeast Asia, the Middle East, in Latin America, in Africa, and Asia. Here also is the loneliness of the old woman next door, the cry of hungry children in our ghettos. And don't forget the angry shouts of black and white militants and anarchists and the majority of middle- and upper-class people anxiously trying to preserve their security with television and money and not get involved. It seems this is our national goal or game: how not to get involved. Who really wants to be God's minister in a world like this if God is not like Christ? Any natural man or woman in his or her right mind would not!

No one would want to join in this kind of caring love unless he had first of all been hugged by the love of God and given the assurance of the Eternal Love ruling all things; for only such a person can believe in the possibility of reconciliation and regeneration of human life. Only he will genuinely pray, "Lord, make me an instrument of Thy peace."

Yes, we must help the hungry to find just plain bread or help them through their own work; for this is the bread of God. Unless we are interested in people—their bodily needs as well as their spiritual—it is unlikely we will convince them we care for them. Of course the deepest needs are not physical but spiritual—the hunger for meaning and hope, the thirst for love and courage. So we are involved in sharing these gifts—call it evangelism or whatever you will. This too is part of prayer and worship.

This is our highest calling—communicating the intention of our Lord and Savior through our deepest intentions shown in our own acts: "That they might have life." To pray and worship therefore requires the readiness to be in some humble but real way another incarnation of the love of Christ.

One of our black mothers in a church in my area told me a thrilling story that belongs here. She said she noticed one of the neighbor boys had not been in church school or worship for two or three Sundays. She asked the boy's mother why and received this reply. "About two months ago both of his grandmothers died within a week. They had taken turns staying with him while I worked. Now he is bereft and refuses to go to church because he says he knows God does not love him or he would not have let his two grandmothers die. I don't know what to tell him." And the young mother herself showed tears in her eyes.

Her neighbor then asked, "Would you tell Mark that I will be glad to be his grandmother if he will let me. This afternoon I will bake some cookies, and you tell him to see me next Sunday."

Next Sunday the little eleven-year-old boy was in his place in church school, and when his neighbor came in, he ran to her and hugged her and she him. "Oh, will you really be my grandmother? Then God does love me, doesn't he?"

This simple involvement does not seem too costly on the surface, but it will take time and energy, which this dear woman does not really have. Nevertheless here is the way to pray and to live. Whether it be going as a missionary to Africa, or as a volunteer helper in the ghetto, or as a minister to the poor-rich on mortgage hill, it costs to care. But "Christianity is to Care" as Baron von Hugel put it in letters to his niece. "Caring is the greatest thing."

Every one of us has a place and a way to lay his life on the line, for there are hungry children, youth, seemingly successful adults, and aged in every place, small or large. There are numberless youth crying out even with their protests for our love and concern. Others are revolting largely because they haven't had anyone to give them love and concern, to listen to them, to care. The following letter from a boy writing to his parents was printed in the *Kansas City Star* at the parents' request—"maybe if we share this letter, it will help other parents."

Dear Folks,

Thank you for everything but I am going to Chicago and try to start some kind of new life.

You ask me why I did those things and why I gave you so much trouble and the answer is easy for me to give you but I am wondering if you will understand.

Remember when I was about 6 or 7 and I wanted you to just listen to me? I remember all the nice things you gave me for Christmas and my birthday and I was real happy with the things for about a week at the time I got them but the rest of the time during the year I really didn't want presents. I just wanted all the time for you to listen to me like I was somebody who felt things too. Because I remember even when I was young I felt things.

But you said you were busy. Mom, you are a wonderful cook. You had everything so clean. You were tired so much from doing all things that would make you busy. But you know something, Mom, I would have liked crackers and peanut butter just as well if you had only sat down with me a little while every day and said to me, "Tell me all about it so I can maybe help you to understand."

I think all the kids who are doing so many things that grown-ups are tearing out their hair worrying about are really looking for somebody who will have time to listen a few minutes and who will really and truly treat them as they would a grown-up who might be useful to them. You know, polite to them. If you folks had ever said, "pardon me," when you interrupted me, I'd have dropped dead.

If anybody asks you where I am, tell them I've gone looking for somebody with time because I've got a lot of things that I want to talk to them about.

Love to all, your son.

How many blind, embittered people are destroying themselves and others! How many youth, as well as those who are older in years, are still poor in love because no one ever really listened to them. No one ever hugged them with accepting love.

Each of us must care deeply about the daily bread of both kinds for others if we would accept our daily bread of meaning, hope, love, and peace. When you pray, "Give us this day our daily bread," remember that your own children, or your wife or husband or friend or the lonely man or woman across the street needs this bread of understanding love—someone to listen to, someone to be friendly, someone to care. And what about the children next door and across the tracks and in the inner city, the children in Calcutta and Lima and Kinshasha and Hong Kong?

No, you can't feed them all, nor can I; but we can find a valid ministry wherever we are. The question is: do you and I encounter the caring love of Christ with such immediacy and adoration that we respond in the joyous prayer of self-giving and the celebration of sacrificial love, so that we may join our caring love with his?

That is the question that will determine the meaning and value of our spiritual disciplines.

WE CANNOT DO IT BY OURSELVES

One thing is sure: no one is self-sufficient. "No man is an island, entire of itself."[14] We are born for community, and belonging is one of our deepest needs. Nowhere is this more true than in the area of spiritual victory over the old self-centered life—the "old man" or "old woman" of self-demands! No one can start *de novo,* isolated from the great stream of human experience in which he may learn from others what a hundred lifetimes on his own could not teach him.

If I am to understand and serve others in caring love, I must understand and know myself. When I pray, "Lead me, but not into temptation," I must have the realism to know what kind of person I am, and not just what I think I am. Without this realistic self-understanding, I may throw myself needlessly into the temptation I cannot or will not resist. Always when an outwardly strong person succumbs to a life-shattering temptation, as happens too often, he doesn't really know himself. Nor do his companions; that is, there is an aloneness, a separation in "the sounds of silence" of people living together without really communicating, "ten thousand people talking without speaking, people hearing without listening."[15]

And so the friends or family say, "What's eating him?" "How could he have done that?" Neither he nor they understand the factors that affect his judgment, the prejudices and group satisfactions to which he is subject, the longing for status and acceptance which has deep roots unrecognized but powerful.

There are things about myself I need to know and understand if I am to grow into the maturity of the new man or woman in Christ; and this self-knowledge is hard to come by and *never* is it found alone. I may find some help through psychology, group therapy, sessions with a psychiatrist, and it must be said with confidence that the Spirit works through these media as well as through the professedly "religious" counselor or friend or group. Most maturity comes in open-minded honesty before the God who knows me as I am—an honesty which may be helped by the group in which I share, but in the last resort the light on who I am at best is given me when I open up every corner of my being to his light. It comes when I cease to trust my own competence or strength, but pray, "I can do all things through him who gives me power. Without him I can do nothing. Show me my false shell and lead me to the person I am in your sight." There is no substitute for this kind of prayer and the celebration in worship that declares jubilantly, "For yours (not mine) *is* the *Kingdom* and the *power* and the *glory, forever* and *ever,* amen!" Only then will my celebration in solitude and in the gathered community enable me to be free really to care intelligently for my family, my church, and my fellow-man.

However, even in the solitude of my personal prayers, as well as in the corporate worship of the church (the koinonia of the early Christians which still exists in powerful reality here and there in the Christian church), I must have group support and guidance, a group in which I join in the acceptance of Christlike disciplines. Here in this matter of our "life together," as Dietrich Bonhoeffer calls it, is the final discipline without which the others will be empty and fruitless. Strangely enough, it is the one discipline most neglected today. Bonhoeffer, though in a Nazi prison awaiting execution, continued strong to the end not only because of his personal meditation and prayer, but because he was supported by a group of loving friends in and out of prison. He wrote,

> This is the test of true meditation and true Christian community. Has the fellowship served to make the individual free, strong, and mature, or has it made him weak and dependent? Has it taken him by the hand for a while in order that he may learn again to walk by himself, or has it made him uneasy and unsure? . . . Blessed is he who is alone in the strength of the fellowship and blessed is he who keeps the fellowship in the strength of aloneness.[16]

This Bonhoeffer knew from experience. The disciplines of personal prayer and meditation must be balanced by the discipline of group silence, fellowship in dialogue and study and celebration through corporate worship. Douglas Rhymes has a sentence that needs to be written in large letters over our churches, schools, homes, and places of work and play.

A society without any disciplines is unable to provide the right environment for freedom, for the resultant anarchy will simply produce a jungle in which the more sensitive go to the wall.[17]

This is what has happened to many homes and churches where young, middle-aged, and older are alone even in what is supposed to be a community. We need the disciplines of a group in which we truly can belong and in which we are able both to listen and to contribute. Without these, we will find, in our society and in our inner lives, an anarchy where the most sensitive go to the wall and the strongest are the most predatory and destructive! How many homes and churches are more likely to resemble a barnyard of squabbling dogs and cats, pigs and chickens than a family where the peace and love of Christ dwells!

We need a *koinonia* as did Jesus and his disciples, whom he chose "that they might be with him." If they needed it we certainly do— this beloved fellowship where we may "speak the truth in love" (Eph. 4:15, RSV), where when one has slipped, all the others join to "restore him in a spirit of gentleness. Look to yourself, lest you too be tempted. Bear one another's burdens" (Gal. 6:1–2, RSV). And yet "each man will have to bear his own load" (Gal. 6:5, RSV).

How do we get such a fellowship? It doesn't just happen, but it is given to those who seek it through disciplined group worship and study, the practice of silence and sharing together, "each one considering the other as better than himself." This requires a corresponding discipline of our individual lives in our times of solitude, for such community of openness and helpfulness to each other requires a genuine humility in the presence of Christ where "we compare ourselves with ourselves and not with one another" (cf. 2 Cor. 10:12–17). Instead we compare ourselves with Christ and the self he knows we are and can be; then only will we be strong and wise enough to share the bread of God, the forgiveness, healing guidance and deliverance God is seeking to bring through us to our brothers.

The warning of Dietrich Bonhoeffer is needed by us all. "Let him who cannot be alone beware of community. . . . Let him who is not in community beware of being alone."[18] For if you attempt to escape from the aloneness in which you see yourself and come to grips with who you are and can be in the presence of God, your presence in the community will only do harm to yourself and the community. On the other hand, unless you are accepted, loved, supported, and guided by the community, your aloneness will bring you to all kinds of illusory leadings and false exaltations or equally false depressions.

The disciplines of solitude and community belong together. Without them and the light and leading they bring, we can never celebrate the agony with the ecstasy and find ourselves able to join in the joy of self-giving love.

> Man . . . will make the choice between arrogant autonomy and loving excentration. This will be the final choice: revolt or adoration of a world.[19]

Colin Morris, president of the United Church of Zambia, has a little book called *Include Me Out!* that points up the choice each of us must make. He wrote it on the very day he received a copy of the *Methodist Recorder* telling about all the minutiae of working out the proposed union between British Methodists and the Church of England. On the very same day a poor starving Zambian died on his doorstep with only a few leaves and a ball of grass in his stomach. As Dr. Morris read and thought about the two events, he wrote, "Include me out!" He does not mean, as he hastens to indicate, "Include me out of union," for he does not believe we should quit working toward a union of our forces as Christians in a pagan world. His theme is rather *include me out of worship or prayer or any other emphasis in the church and in my life that fails to put the deepest needs of people first.* Count me out of worship and prayer that omits the major concerns of compassion, how to share with our neighbors who are starving for want of food and love. Colin Morris's little book contains a classic description of the kind of corporate worship that results when men and women are celebrating the self-giving love of their Lord by joining him in their own action and love.

> The worship of men and women spending themselves in compassionate action would have an air more of desperation than formality. They would stagger into Church utterly drained of goodness, unable to face another day unless their numbed spirits were resensitized and their strength renewed. . . . Every false word

in the service would stick out like a sore thumb . . . the most familiar truth would scorch. They would gulp the bread of Communion like starving men. . . . And they would not casually go through the motions of a ritual expectation of Resurrection on that first day of the week. There would be a heart-stopping suspense as the service progressed. Would they really find a Risen Lord at work in the heart of the tragic mess to which they would have to return?[20]

And they would leave with their spirits renewed and their hearts overflowing, for they had celebrated with the faithful of all ages the presence of *Christus Victor.*

Thus it has been in every day and every time, and thus it will be for those who share in the victory that can truly make this the Age of Aquarius with

> Harmony and understanding,
> Sympathy and trust abounding.
> No more falsehoods or derisions,
> Golden living dreams of visions,
> Mystic crystal revelation,
> And the mind's true liberation.

So let us join with Jesus and his disciples in every age who are caringly involved in self-giving love with the Lord of History:

Count me in wherever Christ is at work in loving reconciliation.

Count me in wherever my brothers and sisters meet for worship and study as we seek together to discover the will of God in these perplexed times.

Count me in when the celebration of the Presence is held, the bread for which I hunger is offered, the wine of love and hope for which I thirst is poured out for me and for all.

Count me in on these set-apart days of solitude where I can get my bearings as I am surrounded by a great cloud of witnesses.

Count me in as I join with others who cry daily, hourly, momently, "Your Kingdom come, your will be done . . . for yours is the Kingdom, the Power and the Glory!"

Count me in with the myriad upon myriads who stand around
the throne of Highest Reality crying, "Alleluia! Amen—Yes"
to Him who reigns in caring love and shall forever reign, "King
of Kings and Lord of Lords forever!"

Then all of life is a sacrament of the unseen reality of God's
presence,; that is, the invisible becomes visible in the experienced
joys and pleasures of the common life, in heroic sacrifices, the
patient bearing of our burdens as we share with him the burdens of
others.
Yes, "awe alone is sterile. But when it is married to sacrificial
love, the fruits of the Spirit begin to appear."[21]

> The God of galaxies—how shall we praise him?
> For so we must, or wither. Yet what word
> Of words? And where to send it, on which night
> Of winter stars, of summer, or by autumn
> In the first evening of the Pleiades?
>
> . . . .
>   oh, what word
> Of words? Let us consider it in terror, [and in joy!]
> And say it [with and] without voice. Praise universes
> Numberless. Praise all of them. Praise Him.[22]

The disciplines required for life in the Age of Aquarius or any
other age are the ones that celebrate the marriage of awe and love,
of worship and work and joyful living, all in the awareness and
response to the God who in Christ is hugging us and the whole
universe unto himself and calling us to join in the glorious celebration.

NOTES

1. From an ancient collect used over many centuries of church
worship.
2. From a paper presented in Geneva, Switzerland, August 1969.
3. Ibid.
4. James F. White, *The Worldliness of Worship* (New York: Oxford
University Press, 1967), p. 20.
5. Peter L. Berger, *A Rumor of Angels* (Garden City, N.Y.:
Doubleday, 1969), jacket review.
6. Neither Peter Berger nor this author is appealing for a return

to a view of the supernatural that "breaks in" to our natural world, but rather for the supernatural as arising "out of" and therefore as the *source and heart* of the so-called natural world.

7. Hammarskjöld, *Markings,* p. 122.

8. Aulén, *Dag Hammarskjöld's White Book.* p. 119.

9. Thomas Merton, *Seeds of Contemplation* (Norfolk, Connecticut: New Directions Books by James Laughlin, 1949), p. 60.

10. Chandler W. Sterling, *The Holroyd Papers* (London: Bartholomew House, Ltd., 1969).

11. Ibid., pp. 263–64.

12. Ibid., p. 268.

13. "Abba," *The Fruits of the Spirit, Light of Christ, Abba* (New York: David Mckay, 1956; *Abba* copyright 1940), p. 24.

14. John Donne, "Devotions," XVII.

15. Simon and Garfunkel.

16. Dietrich Bonhoeffer, *Life Together* (New York: Harper & Bros., 1954), pp. 88–89.

17. Douglas Rhymes, *Prayer in the Secular City,* p. 45.

18. Bonhoeffer, p. 77.

19. Pierre Teilhard de Chardin, *The Future of Man* (New York: Harper & Row, 1964), p. 19.

20. Colin Morris, *Include Me Out!* (Nashville: Abingdon, 1968), pp. 36–37.

21. Underhill, p. 25.

22. Mark Van Doren, "The God of Galaxies," *Collected and New Poems 1924–1963* (New York: Hill and Wang, 1963), pp. 437–38.